CONTROVERSY CONFUSION
AND CATASTROPHE

Controversy Confusion and Catastrophe
Catholicism in the Wake of Vatican II

JOHN FRAWLEY

*Controversy is the engine room of argument and
properly predicated argument is the machinery of progress*

Modotti Press

Published by Modotti Press, an imprint of Connor Court Publishing Pty Ltd

Copyright © John Frawley 2015

ALL RIGHTS RESERVED. This book contains material protected under International and Federal Copyright Laws and Treaties. Any unauthorised reprint or use of this material is prohibited. No part of this book may be reproduced or transmitted in any form or by any means, electronic or mechanical, including photocopying, recording, or by any information storage and retrieval system without express written permission from the publisher.

PO Box 224W
Ballarat VIC 3350
sales@connorcourt.com
www.connorcourt.com

ISBN: 9781925138627 (pbk.)

Cover design by Maria Giordano, photo taken from istockphoto.com

Printed in Australia

Contents

Preface vi
1. The Seeds of Confusion 1
2. Human Life 9
3. A Sacramental Church 18
4. Church Authority 24
5. Ecumenism 31
6. Liturgy 39
7. A Great Catastrophe 50
8. Human Sexuality 57
9. Contraception 71
10. Stewardship of Procreation 84
11. Life-creating Technology 91
12. Death and New Life 96
13. The New Millennium 100
14. The Great Paradox 106
15. The Healing 113
16. "Such is life" 123
    A Last Word 127

PREFACE

In the light of the signature Australian characteristics of individualism, egalitarianism and disrespect for authority, it was perhaps to be expected that Catholicism's teachings on those matters which address the morality of human life and freedom to live it as one wishes would produce conflict. Modern Australia and Catholicism are in conflict both within the Church and in society at large with catastrophic consequences. Such turmoil has accelerated over the past 50 years following the Second Vatican Council despite the Council's intention to bring renewal and some reform which would see Catholicism flourish with enhanced relevance in the coming new millennium. Renewal and reformation did not follow the Council and Catholicism has failed to flourish.

With the on-going dissatisfaction and disruption that has marked the past 50 years in the life of the Catholic Church, it is reasonable to examine what the Second Vatican Council (Vatican II) has achieved and what it has failed to achieve for Catholicism, and whether or not there is validity in the echoing clamour for renewal and reform. Such examination properly demands an assessment of the Vatican II documents together with those moral teachings applied to the living of human life which are the major drivers of the demands for change. While this is written from an Australian perspective, the problems for the modern Catholic Church are similar throughout Western society and transcend cultural and national differences.

Immersed in argument and lost in the midst of experimental and developmental exploratory excursions into adulthood was perhaps one of the most valuable experiences of early university life. These hopefully world-changing deliberations were exchanged between an exclusive Catholic educated clique of males, Australian born and derived within three generations or less mainly from an Irish immigrant origin. We were also part of the first generation of Australian Catholics, unlike the generations before us, educated to enter the universities rather than the public service or a trade and to be nurtured in the bosom of the Australian Labor Party and the trade unions. Not only had we achieved good academic credentials but each one of us could recite the Catholic catechism backwards. Occasionally, someone would become rebellious and question the authority of the Church of St Peter, instituted by God the Creator himself in the miraculous personage of a Judean, celibate miracle worker, one Jesus of Nazareth, singular amongst humankind not only as God-made-man but equally remarkably as the product of a virgin birth.

As we warmed to the contrasts and freedoms of university life, Protestants became part of the late night intellectual excursions and eventually, too, even women were admitted. We found that some women were, surprisingly, not a lot different in attitude from the men. Protestant women were not quite so Marian and possessed an intriguing mystery that the Catholics didn't, perhaps because we assumed a less than righteous attitude to sexuality. After more than occasional false assumptions it was surprising to find that many Protestants were possessed of a sexual morality similar to that of Catholics without any specific knowledge or privilege bestowed on them by the teachings of the Holy Catholic Church.

We discovered, too, unexpectedly, that many Protestants and even humanist atheists possessed a morality that put some of we catechised soldiers of Catholicism in the shade. I imagine we had no concept at that time of the notion of the natural law, the genesis of that instinctive, built-in human trait that bestows an appreciation of right and wrong, something that the catechism did not embrace as far as I can remember. It didn't matter though because we were chosen, we were the lucky ones, we were right, even perhaps disturbingly righteous, members of the only genuine Christian Church. We were the shining moral examples of the Judeo-Christian ethic, the very foundation of Western society and all that was good about it. Our Catholic Christianity had a higher guiding authority far superior to the common or garden Protestant parson or English monarch, the villains in the sectarian pantomimes of those times.

And then it happened. Most of we university co-travellers graduated in 1962 and during the few years immediately thereafter as the Second Vatican Council deliberated on the direction of the Catholic Church in the coming new millennium. Sixteen new papal approved pieces of policy, the Vatican II documents, dribbled out of the Vatican enclave with the triumphal proclamation that the doors and windows were opened wide in a renaissance that would carry Catholicism to liberation from its ageing shackles, irrelevancies in this modern world. Catholics everywhere cheered as the light shone in through the windows and the old flew out the doors. However, the light streaming in through the open windows did not shine on the liberating changes that large sections of the Catholic communion had expected, changes based largely on speculation and personal desires, rather than an identified need for the well-being of the Church.

In consequence, much did fly out the now open doors, including priests, members of religious orders, laymen and women, the rich liturgy of the Church that had contributed some of the most magnificent, uplifting, sacred music ever written, and commitment to teaching and guiding moral authority. This was not a new Catholicism as many had expected. Virtually no fundamental moral teaching was changed. The catechism that had cemented us to Catholicism essentially hadn't changed in a way that would redefine Catholicism. The Council had undertaken a refreshing episode of long overdue spring cleaning. The summer that followed, however, was not the expected idyll but rather one spoiled by storm and fire. In the wake of Vatican II came controversy and confusion of a magnitude that has brought near societal irrelevance and large scale destruction and distrust to the Catholic Church in the Western world. Such controversy and confusion has arisen not because of changes in belief or basic teaching and theology but from widescale misinterpretation of the Vatican II documents and their intent. It would seem that sections of the clergy and a vast number of Catholics have made their own interpretations, usually matching their own hopes and desires, despite the vast majority of the Catholic laity never having read the Vatican II documents or heard any discussion of them in the public domain or in their local parishes.

Controversy is never a matter of concern since in it resides the capacity for argument and an imperative to achieve resolution. The current controversies confronting Catholicism are solvable but when confusion reigns, progress and healing are nigh impossible. The overwhelming imperative facing the post-Vatican II Holy Catholic Church is the resolution of confusion. Much of the modern day confusion in Catholicism stems from the fact that since Vatican II, for reasons which escape understanding, the authoritative Catholic Church, Christ's chosen teaching vehicle, would seem to have abandoned the education of its people with catastrophic consequences. Those born after Vatican II concluded are now in the age group of infancy to 50 years, poorly educated in the teachings and theology of Catholicism. However, since most young people are too preoccupied with matters other than religion it is highly likely that many confused Catholics, teenagers at the time of the Second Vatican Council, are now 65-70 years old. Only those old faithfuls aged over 65-70 years grace the pews in numbers these days and one would have to suggest that they are not all stupid and uninformed. They do, after all, possess the longest life experience, have remained faithful to the Church and include peoples from all walks of life, levels of secular education and many of prominence in society at large. Indeed, it is far more likely that they represent the remnants of the educated Catholic layman and from the majority of Catholics who are not confused in this modern world.

The major controversies and confusions that accompany Catholic teaching are related in the main to human birth, death and sexuality. Secondary derivatives of these are found in feminist interests and matters of Church authority. All of these have a fundamental substrate best assembled under the generic, human life. Perhaps the resolution of the controversies and confusions of today's Catholics and those opponents of the Catholic Church, whether Catholic, Protestant, pagan or atheist, might be found in the understanding of the Catholic perception of human life. Resolution will, of course, not be found by all, simply because to understand the Catholic position, it is fundamental to believe in the existence of a God Creator and to acknowledge the imperfections of the greatest of all God's creation, the sage human being, self-eulogised as the species *homo sapiens,* the intelligent man.

To achieve resolution and a resurrection of Catholicism, it is also necessary to express the Catholic position in language which a theologically uneducated lay person can understand and apply to the ordinariness of everyday life, rather than in a created, quasi-academic language which is fully understood only by its creators and in consequence bestows on them a mysticism which empowers authority while perpetuating ignorance or uncertainty in those not privy to the language used. The magisterial language encapsulating the teachings and theology of the Catholic Church eludes the understanding of the vast body of average lay people who constitute the Church, particularly the young. In what is written here, I have tried to eliminate such language in the quest for easy comprehension and might indeed generate further confusion or be dismissed as a theological ignoramus. "Keep it simple, stupid" is, however, to be preferred to the alternative "Keep the simple stupid."

A common question put to writers is "Why did you write this"? My reply would be that it was my hope to express the Catholic teachings on human life in a simple language sufficient to dispel confusion and promote sound discussion in the hope of stimulating progress and understanding of a Church which in the last half century has shaken its very foundations to the core and, some might say, lost its way. Despair, distrust, detraction and self-serving authoritarianism, the antitheses of hope and trust, have raised their ugly heads in recent troubled times and alienated many erstwhile devoted Catholics. But if nothing else, the Catholic Church is above all else one of hope and trust in God, both fundamental to the Christian way of life. What is written here is dependent on belief. To those alienated Catholics and those who do not believe in a Creator God, I hope that should such souls read these musings, they might glean some understanding of the basis of some Catholic philosophy, teaching and dogma as understood by a simple layman who, despite challenging life experiences, still believes.

Much of what is written here will in itself bring controversy, confusion and bitter criticism from some or perhaps many. I should point out at the outset that I have intended to account for Catholic teaching as it exists at the time of writing. Some of the controversial issues such as ordination of women to the priesthood, human life creation technologies, priestly celibacy, contraception, abortion, feminism and homosexuality are discussed, not with any intent other than to explain the basis of current Catholic teaching to those who find nothing but confusion in these matters. Further, it is not my intention to exert any influence for change through these musings while recognising that change under the administration of Pope Francis may well modify some of the current teachings and that some changes are urgently needed if Catholicism is to grow or indeed survive in the new millennium. I trust, however, that those teachings besieged by controversy and confusion will nevertheless be clear and easy to understand and thus stimulate productive debate and progress towards a rejuvenated Catholic Church. It is necessary also to re-affirm that this commentary does not embody the full spectrum of Catholic teaching, only those teachings which relate to human life matters of controversy and confusion, and has no pretensions as another catechism of the Catholic Church nor as a theological treatise.

JEF, January 2015

All biblical quotes in this work are from the *Good News Bible, Catholic Study Edition*.

1

THE SEEDS OF CONFUSION

Be on your guard against false prophets;
they come to you looking like sheep on the outside,
but on the inside they are really wolves.
You will know them by what they do.

Matt 7:15-16

There is no harvest without the sowing of the seed

Modern Western society largely dismisses morality as meaningless, nothing but an imposition on the freedom of the intelligent, progressive, educated human being. In consequence, a large scale abandonment of adherence to Catholic Church teaching and a ridiculing of its authority have arisen and proved very difficult to counter. The Catholic Church finds itself faced with falling participation in Church life and practice and falling numbers of ordained priests from the Western world. There are many who would say that this comes from the perceived injustice of the imposition on its people of Church teachings on the morality of issues such as sexuality, contraception, abortion, euthanasia and modern life-creating technologies, or even more so perhaps, from a refusal to change those teachings to fit in with the world at large.

Also driving demand for renewal and reform of some Catholic teaching is the feminist agenda which cries out for gender equality through female ordination to priesthood and a democratic place for women in the authority structure of the Catholic Church. Hand in hand with the perceived intransigence of the current administration of the Church to accede to these demands is the damaging sexual abuse of children that pervades all institutions and has not spared the Catholic Church whose efforts to maintain its image by keeping this scandal from public scrutiny over many years has inflicted great damage on its credibility as a custodian and prescriber of human moral behaviour. There is little if any forgiveness extended to the Church in this environment.

Human society constantly evolves, sometimes imperceptibly over generations, and sometimes with the dramatic confluence of momentous events which in their often unheralded arrival bring great disruption and change. Such a confluence was seen, for example, during the enormous tragedy and loss of life that came with World War II. The loss of life in that conflagration was not entirely due to bomb, bullet and bayonet. A vast death toll accompanied the lack of nutrition caused by the conflict and the subsequent invasion of vulnerable human beings by the lethal armies of bacteria and viruses for which the world possessed no counter armamentarium. Untreatable infection from contamination of non-life-threatening wounds and frailty of health claimed many lives, both military and civilian, until the Australian Nobel Prize winner Howard Florey, working at Oxford University, offered his production system for penicillin to the Americans.

Winston Churchill had dismissed the development of penicillin in England as a secondary and unimportant consideration to winning the war against the Axis forces of Fascism and thus abandoned the development of perhaps the greatest British contribution to human society in the 20th century. Penicillin became available to the American forces soon after and saved many lives wounded in combat and the millions of civilians, particularly children, who would otherwise have died from incurable bacterial infection. So dramatic was the impact of penicillin in its confluence with war that its production soon accelerated and penicillin became available to the world at large changing human society forever. In its wake, diseases such as pneumonia, rheumatic fever, scarlet fever and septicaemia that had scourged human life from time immemorial were no longer threats and human society was irretrievably changed for the better.

In the immediate years after World War II, other events, independent of each other, were destined in their confluence to change human society and were the prelude to the rapidly changing human world of the last half of the 20th century and remain extant to this day. The post–war invention of a convenient and effective oral contraceptive precipitated radical changes in fundamental philosophy which have threatened the health of Christian Western society with a damaging moral malaise. The widespread introduction of "the pill" was soon followed by radical feminism, the so-called sexual revolution and the attempted modernisation of Catholicism in this brave new world by the Second Vatican Council. Rather than benefitting from this confluence of world changing events in the 20 years after the war as followed the advent of penicillin, Western Christian society seems to be progressively deteriorating with increasing conflict, loss of ethical practice in human relationships, war, domestic violence and the destruction or diminution of societal institutions which have served human society very successfully for centuries, notably amongst these, Christian marriage and family, medicine, education and law. In the wake of this turbulent confluence of societal changes, the Catholic Church has found itself in conflict with society at large and especially with many of its own people.

The development of a pill capable of preventing human ovulation and thus, the creation of human life, clashed with the teaching of the Catholic Church. To deliberately interfere with human life creation by the artificial control of human conception was contrary to the natural law and consequently not permissible in the living of a moral life. This morality was at the time adhered to, accepted and unchallenged, at least in the public domain, by the vast majority of Catholics and large sections of non-Catholic Christianity. The aesthetics of an oral contraceptive very quickly saw its ascendancy as the preferred modern form of contraception. Its widespread use removed the fear and stigma of unwanted pregnancy without the tawdriness and embarrassment of some other forms of artificial contraception and the disastrous consequences of clandestine abortion by untrained non-medical abortionists. "The pill" encouraged an environment of freedom in sexual practice, soon followed by enhancement of its pleasures through a drug-induced euphoria and female aggressive promiscuity promoted by radical feminism. The so-called sexual revolution had begun. And as with any revolution that challenges human society, open warfare would follow, the proponents being the culture of freedom from moral constraint, sexual or otherwise, and Catholicism whose teachings on human life morality were seen by many as the very antithesis of freedom. Similarly, Christianity generally and its reflection in the structures and civil law of Western society came under challenge in the modern world.

The vast changes in Christian Western society and Catholicism happen to have gained momentum in the years following the Second Vatican Council convened in the years 1963-1965. This confluence, however, does not accord a causal or a contributory responsibility for the changes in these institutions to the Council. Rather, the progressive destruction of Western society and Catholicism relates in the main to the sexual revolution with its promotion of profligate sexual lifestyles, normalisation of homosexual activities and a militant brand of indulgent feminism which trashed the basic stabilising foundations of Christian Western society, namely, womanhood in its roles of mothering and nurturing a family and the institution of marriage. This revolution promoted not only sexual freedom but also the destruction of inconvenient human life through abortion and, more recently, euthanasia. Feminism removed the pedestal on which Western society and Catholicism placed womanhood with the consequence that women became objects for sexual gratification and lost respect – women were not special anymore. Both Western society and Catholicism were slow to address this revolution and to openly maintain and defend their ethics and principles in the face of demands for radical changes designed in the main to serve the individual rather than the society. Both it would seem were afraid of loss of face or criticism in the modern world.

The apparent inflexible exclusion of Catholics from participation in the sexual freedoms of the new post-war world that the contraceptive pill permitted was seen as archaic and unacceptable in an evolving modern world. This, together with other irritations such as priestly celibacy, unquestioning subservience to a hierarchical Church authority and the rising star of radical feminism sowed the seeds of demand for change in the Catholic Church which was perceived in many quarters to be falling behind post-war modernity and becoming entrenched in an irrelevant past. The demands for change were essentially for changes in those moral tenets of Catholic teaching which interfered with perceived freedoms and rights of individuals in the living of human life. Such demands in the main reflected a personal selfishness, something of the opposite to what Christ expected of his followers. Attempts to reform the divine intent of Christ's Church were bound to bring some disruption.

The necessity to meet this modern world, examine its edicts and implications and to define the moral position of the Catholic Church was recognised by Pope John XXIII (1958-1963) who convened the Second Vatican Council, a conclave of the Church hierarchy acting in response to its people and opened to opinion and advice offered by both male and female lay persons and members of religious communities both Catholic and non-Catholic, in a quest to bring Catholicism as a relevancy into this new age. (Voting on the recommendations of the Council was not open to all participating delegates but confined to those delegates in the Church hierarchy, essentially those clergy ranked bishop and above, under the overall authority of the Pope).

When the Council was convened, it became obvious that within the Catholic Church hierarchy there existed both conservatives who shunned any concept of change and progressives who demanded change in fundamental, immutable aspects of Catholic teaching, with a large centre faction open to genuine debate. After some progressives threatened to boycott the Council, Pope John addressed the clash between these opposing factions in the words, "... the essence of Catholic doctrine and morals would not change to suit modern tastes".

This proved to be the case when the Council released the documentation of its deliberations. One of the major features of the Vatican II documents is the ratification of existing moral teaching with virtually no fundamental change. The major changes which did come were simply in the interests of better housekeeping, ease of involvement of the laity in the liturgy and the recognition that Christianity was not the exclusive property of Catholicism. Some of these simple changes have proved counter-productive quite apart from the disappointment that came with the failure to liberalise teaching to suit the modern world. If anything, the Vatican II documents confirmed the truth and enduring nature of established teaching over the 2,000 years preceding the Council. It is not unreasonable to suggest that perhaps the major message of Vatican II may be that the practices of the modern world are the things that require reform and renewal rather than the moral teachings and practice of Catholicism.

After its deliberations from October 1962 to December 1965, the Second Vatican Council produced sixteen documents defining Catholicism for the modern world. These documents had overwhelming support from the 2,625 voting council delegates. Indeed, the most controversial of the documents with the greatest opposition amongst the delegates, the *Decree on Religious Freedom, Dignitatis Humanae,* was approved with a majority of 1,773 (1,997 to 224). The Council promise of reform enjoyed widespread support by an excited Catholic laity around the world as well as amongst many non-Catholic people. The Vatican II documents are in the main clear and precise. Despite this, it would seem, the Council has generated much distress for the Church, not so much because of what the documents proclaim but largely perhaps because of what they did not proclaim.

Much of the distress has its origins in people who urge for change of basic doctrine to accommodate their ideas, not necessarily those of the Church as a community. In the light of the overwhelming approval by the delegates of all of the documents, including a very clear articulation of the nature of authority in the Church, it is a matter of some concern that so many Catholics ignored the statements of the Council and have chosen for the last 50 years to pursue their own agendas, demanding renewal and reformation. Many of these demands fly in the face of authority and long-established moral teaching. Reform groups clamouring for renewal or implementation of what they believe is the true intent of the Second Vatican Council cry out for a democratic Church, rule of the people, by the people, for the people, not the prescription recorded in sacred scripture as Christ's preferred option for his Church on Earth. Christ in his life was not the model for, and his Church has never been, a democracy. And yet, the Catholic Church has endured for two millennia despite many ups and downs.

Quite apart from the mind-numbing pride, the underlying character of all of these militant self-interest groups almost certainly lies in personal disappointment in the failure of the Council to change fundamental Church teaching. This may seem a harsh assessment. However, the one enduring fact of human nature is that the human being reacts most enthusiastically, passionately and, indeed, vehemently against those interests which impose upon or deny personal preferences, desires or freedoms. Therein lies one of democracy's major flaws. Democracy carries within itself the very seed of its own potential destruction, the all-powerful "self" of the people. Christ's life and the signature of the Church he founded is not "self" but "selflessness". It may be that the Catholic Church has endured because it is a non-democratic institution guided by a supreme authority rather than a democracy serving human rather than spiritual well-being.

The modern day reformers have magnified those issues peripheral to moral teaching and claim that a recalcitrant Church hierarchy has failed to implement the true spirit of the Council. There are those who bring their own interpretations to various aspects of Church life which have had the effect in some practice of replacing the divine with the human and the sacred with the profane, destroying the sacred liturgy and an appreciation in the modern day Catholics of God in their midst in a sacramental church. This has secularised Catholicism and changed many of its places of worship into community meeting halls where reverence for the presence of God therein is sadly abandoned, essentially an abandonment of sacramentality, the very signature of Catholicism. Since most conflict relates to matters of living human life, it is necessary to have an understanding of Catholic teaching on what human life is.

2
HUMAN LIFE

Hanc meam artem profitebor cum pietate et sanctitatae
The Hippocratic Oath

The essence of creation

The mausoleum-like building at the top of the gentle slope behind the biggest hospital I had ever seen loomed as the temple of my youthful ambition. Partly obscured by a parkland of stately eucalypts, its facade boasted massive classical Greek columns resting on the summit of a broad stand of stairs, an impressive portal of entry to an otherwise undecorated block of red bricks, crowned by a copper dome, oxidised green with time and weather. I stood on the concourse, a disbelieving 17-year-old country boy, a foreigner in the big city, standing on the cusp of a dream surveying the Medical School of the University of Queensland. This foreboding edifice draped in the mystery of the unknown was to be my hall of learning for at least the next six years if academic fortune was kind.

On the heavy sandstone architrave surmounting the entrance doors of the Medical School an engraved Latin inscription welcomed me with what was expected of all who entered here. For a Catholic schoolboy of the mid-20th century, the Latin posed little problem in its translation, something which largely eluded those who had not studied this archaic language and, I suspect, entered these hallowed halls draped in inspirations of multiple origins, ranging from a desire for future prestige to financial security, from the gaining of scientific knowledge to the thrill of discovery, from empathy with human suffering to personal satisfaction and some perhaps seeking the romance of Hollywood's fabulous portrayals of the healing art.

When I entered beneath the Latin into a strange new world, my perception of human life changed. The Latin demanded of we raw medical students a lifelong commitment, a covenant with the sick, "I will practise this my art with purity and holiness."

The Hippocratic Oath was written in 460 BC by a pagan practitioner of the art of medicine nearly half a millennium before Jesus of Nazareth, the seed of Christianity, was born. Hippocrates was one of those Greek scholars, who with others like Aristotle and Socrates in other academic disciplines, fashioned a world that evolved into the most civilised culture of the times. Myth, superstition and inhumanity were progressively dispelled with the coming of the disciplined thought of philosophy and logic, the discovery of scientific truth in physics and mathematics and the recognition of the capability of the aesthetics of architecture, the arts and the humanities to nurture the human spirit. With truth, knowledge and the law came the ordering of society along democratic principles, somewhat different from those of today's democracies, but nonetheless admitting the people's opinions. Even though these ancient humanists paid homage to a host of pagan gods, in some ways they approached the ideal of Christianity. Indeed, not only did the Hippocratic Oath strike me as being very catholic[1] but also very Catholic.

For a young man educated in dogmatic, catechetical Catholicism tempered with a good dose of Irish paganism and occasional irrationality, the concept that an ancient pagan culture, that had never heard of Jesus of Nazareth or the Christianity that he established, saw human life and its stewardship as a matter of purity and holiness, that is, of sanctity, came as a difficult concept to embrace. Sanctity (holiness of life, saintliness, sacredness, being hallowed, demanding reverence, inviolable) was certainly something beyond most ordinary

---

[1] catholic, adj = universal; of interest or use to all men; all-embracing, of wide sympathies, broad-minded, tolerant. *The Concise Oxford Dictionary of Current English.*

people. And yet the Catholic Church proclaimed the sanctity of human life even with all its shortcomings and propensity for evil in perhaps greater proportion than its aspiration to goodness, purity or holiness. The surprising discovery that indeed a pagan Hippocrates predated the Catholic Church in the perception of what was essentially the sanctity of human life demanded radical realignment of my exclusively Catholic view of the world and all that it contained which threatened the alienating possibility of disillusionment in the unravelling of learnt-by-rote tenets.

There is little doubt that the ancient pagan Greeks placed high value on human life and had also recognised the fundamental existence of a dimension in the human being that transcended all other life. The Hellenic philosophers gave credence to the spirit of humanity; they discovered or vocalised what Christianity calls a soul; they respected the awful wonder that is human life; they understood that human life is special, that it is precious and should not be violated. Ancient Greece, emerging from a world of barbarism towards civilisation, can claim authorship of the concept of the value of human life and the existence of an abstract human spirit.

However, in its selectivity as to which human life deserved such recognition it disqualified itself from any claims on the notion of the sanctity of human life as understood in Christianity, even though Hippocrates might have used the words purity and holiness, implying sanctity, in his sworn covenant with the sick. It is clear that Catholicism cannot claim ownership or authorship of the concept of the value of human life. Paganism in various guises from the ancient civilisations to the present day recognises a fundamental quality attached to human life as opposed to all other life. Herein is the expression of the natural law, that innate possession by all humanity, regardless of any particular denominational religious adherence, of a knowledge of right and wrong, an innate morality, needing no proof or explanation.

Catholicism can, however, claim ownership of the concept of the sanctity of human life in that Catholicism embodies this concept in its theology, teaching that human life is in itself holy, sanctified, approaching Godliness, deserving of deferential respect and different from all other life on this planet. Catholic teaching enshrines the notion that God has created all that we human beings know and perceive: the universe, Earth, all living things, animal and vegetable, all the elements. This does not necessarily mean that God has specifically and as an isolated, stand-alone event at a particular pin-point in time, created individually each flower that blooms, each blade of grass, each living creature from the unicellular amoeba to the multicellular, multifunctional supreme being of all, the human being.

What God has created are the basic procreative mechanisms through which all life comes, from the human being to the lowliest of primitive unicellular life, animal and plant alike. Each individual life is the product of a self-perpetuating process through which life continues in a particular species across the eons of time. For the human being, this mechanism for the continuation of human life has been placed under the stewardship of human beings themselves and Catholic teaching defines what that obligation of stewardship demands of each individual human being, denominationally Catholic or otherwise, believer or non-believer.

Thus, God does not directly design and create John Smith with his red hair, blue eyes and bowed legs at 0200 hours on Monday 10 May 2012. This John Smith comes from the sexual union of a man and a woman with particular so-called genetic characteristics. This union of man and woman results in the fusion of a cell from each, a spermatozoon from the man and an ovum from the woman. From this fusion grows a new organism made up of characteristics reliant on genes (genetic determinators) from both the man and the woman in equally shared proportions so that the new life produced is essentially a replica of half the woman and half the man, the sex of the ensuing life depending on whether the fusion inherits an X or the corresponding Y chromosome from the male sexual partner, a female being genetically XX and a male, XY. Thus the new life may be a male or female human being with the blue eyes of the male, the red hair of the female and perhaps the bowed legs of a member of an earlier generation which produced the sexual partners themselves; that is, the generation of grandparents or earlier. It is this mechanism that God has created and through intermediaries, a man and woman, God has created John Smith. It is a mechanism replicated throughout the animal world and, with variations, in all species of living things, sometimes with the aid of intermediaries necessary to make the fusion of male and female cells possible; for example, the bee as an intermediary in fertilisation through pollen transference from male to female plants. For all organic life, abnormalities associated with disease or other unfavourable environmental conditions, can produce a life that is disordered, undeveloped or imperfect in some way, as happens, for example, through mutation or damage to the determining genes. That does not mean, however, that God the Creator has made a mistake, anymore than it is God's mistake if a perfectly beautiful and normal human being or, indeed, a human life still in the protective nurturing of a mother's womb, is struck down in an accident and killed, invalided, deformed or deprived of mental capacity as a result.

If this is indeed the truth of creation, how does the human being differ from any other living organism on the planet? How can human life claim sanctification as proclaimed by the Catholic Church? Would not all life be equally sanctified if God has created a procreative mechanism for life in all living species, animal or vegetable? In these questions resides the core of Catholic belief on human life creation. Catholic teaching affirms that God does not leave his creation of the human being entirely to the fate of the genetic results of a union of cells from an individual man and woman engaging in procreative sexual union. The human being is different from all other procreative life, in that God, who possesses a human dimension evidenced in the person of Jesus of Nazareth, does intervene when human life comes into being through sexual union and makes that human being his own. God intervenes in that he bestows on each human being, and in no other living creature, a spiritual dimension, an immortal and everlasting spirit, a soul, that transcends human life and is destined after human death to enter an eternity of spiritual life in God's presence. It is within this context that Catholic belief accepts that all human beings are created equal, in God's image, possessing, like Christ, a human as well as an immortal spiritual component of life, destined like Christ to a resurrection after human death as a spiritual being existing for eternity in God the Creator's presence.

In this elemental Christ-like nature exists the holiness or sanctity of all human life which forms the basis of Catholic teaching on human life. All human beings are created equal. All human beings are extraordinary and superior to all other created life. All human life is to be respected regardless of its multiple failings. All human life is God's favoured creation and this Creator, this artist, loves all that he has made regardless of race or creed. It is this fundamental premise regarding the nature of human life that dictates Catholic morality on issues such as racism, slavery, trafficking in human life, prostitution and treatment of refugees. Again, it is the same premise that dictates Catholic morality on all forms of abuse committed against the sanctity of human life such as murder, violent assault in all its forms, drunkenness, mind altering drug use or putting life at risk through reckless behaviour, for example, by disobeying traffic regulations or performing surgical procedures without proper training or for purposes other than the cure of disease or physical abnormality.

Declaring through its moral tenets the obligation of all humanity as the instruments of creation to exercise responsible stewardship of human life, the Catholic Church conflicts with human sexual self-indulgence and in so doing produces controversy and, for some, confusion, expressed as rebellion against an oppressive, authoritarian Church. Thus, Catholicism and modern society are in conflict over sexuality, contraception, abortion, modern scientific life creating technologies and surrogacy, all part of the clamour for renewal and change from various factions in the post-Vatican II Church and, in varying degrees, reasons for the abandonment of Catholicism by numbers of Catholics. Catholicism similarly is in conflict with radical feminism which sees Catholic teachings centring on human life creation as anti-woman in so much as the feminists consider that they alone hold dominion over pregnancy. It is the woman's body that houses a pregnancy and, therefore, woman alone possesses the right to manage that pregnancy even though that management might involve the destruction of human life by abortion. The clamour from the reformers and proponents of Catholic renewal for change in the Church's position regarding various aspects of human sexuality and the creation of human life is driven, it is claimed, by the spirit of Vatican II, something which in their opinions has not guided the Papacy for the last 50 years. Rather, the spirit has preferred to guide a fleet of often self-appointed Catholic spokespersons in the various media, ex-priests and ex-religious, apostate bishops, priests, members of the Catholic laity and deluded feminists.

Recognition of the sanctity of human life formed the basis of ethics embodied in the Judeo-Christian ethic, the defining basis of our Western civilisation, often vocalised as the immortal declaration by Western leaders since its birth as the United States Declaration of Independence, introduced by Thomas Jefferson in 1776 and made famous around the world through the words of Martin Luther King Jr, "I have a dream that one day this nation will rise up, live out the true meaning of its creed: 'We hold these truths to be self-evident, that all men are created equal, that they are endowed by their creator with certain unalienable rights, that among these are Life, Liberty and the Pursuit of Happiness'... ". We in Western society have challenged the immortality of the immortal declaration and ignored its concept over the last half century. Western society has forgotten or chooses to ignore the sanctity of human life.

By its very nature, civilisation in its evolution progressively excludes barbarity and in its decline is correspondingly encroached upon by the barbarity it replaced, somewhat analogous with the built civilisation of the Inca nation now overrun by the jungle it replaced. In Western civilisation today, the law, essential to the ordering of society, has abandoned its basic civilising ideals of protection of human life and societal stability. Through legislation that seeks freedom to destroy human life by abortion and euthanasia and threatens societal stability by seeking to destroy marriage and abolish the natural law through permitting the amoral use of science in the creative processes of human life, the law has abandoned the very civilising influence which it contributed to Western civilisation. In consequence, Western society is progressively declining to a level marked by the abandonment of truth, the dumbing down of education, the abandonment of Jefferson's self-evident truths and the elevation of moral wrongs to human rights. Very few modern day Catholics understand the pivotal role of the sanctity of human life in Catholic philosophy and teaching. And when Catholics don't understand it, it might be expected that neither will the secular humanists, the atheists, the agnostics, the vast majority of Protestants or the army of ever poised critics.

In essence, there is no ordinary human life. All human life is extraordinary and created equal in the eyes of the Creator. All human life has two components, a spiritual, immortal life which is equal and without favour in any individual and a physical, mortal life which varies from person to person and contributes to the human diversity and inequalities that we all know and acknowledge. All human life is precious and extraordinary. Every human being is special regardless of humanity's multiple failings, dreadful personalities and propensity for sheer bastardry. Hippocrates knew that, two and a half thousand years ago. All human beings know that instinctively. Even our neighbours in all species of the animal kingdom instinctively know the value of the life they produce through their various procreative acts. Their entire lives revolve around the preservation of that life that they are capable of passing on to the generations to come. Australia in an enduring sadness has forgotten the Christian meaning of human life itself. Perhaps that is understandable when human beings are not only the most supreme of all created creatures but also the most flawed, a consequence of free will, another of the human being's unique gifts from the Creator which some do not always treasure.

3

A Sacramental Church

Hail, Mary, full of grace, the Lord is with you!
Blessed are you amongst women and blessed is
the fruit of your womb, Jesus.

Prayer based on Luke 1:28-35

God and humanity: an inseparable partnership

To understand Catholic philosophy and teaching is to understand that the Catholic Church is a sacramental Church, singularly different in company with its theological equivalents[2] from all other Christian denominations. Such an understanding is a necessity if the modern Church is to be renewed or reformed. According to the accounts of the public life of Jesus of Nazareth, the Christ, in the writings of his followers, the New Testament authors, the evangelists Matthew, Mark, Luke and John, it seems that his teachings gained popular support while instilling suspicion, controversy, confusion and even fear in those in authority. This is not surprising when these writings contained eyewitness accounts of disease and suffering cured by his word or by the touch of his hand, of his compassion and love for all men, of his exhortation to love one's enemies and turn the other cheek, of his humble acceptance of a Creator God whom he called his

---

2 There are some 22 Eastern Catholic Churches, autonomous and self-governing but in full communion with the Catholic Church. The Second Vatican Council addressed these Churches in the documents, *Orientalium Ecclesiarum, Lumen Gentium* and *Unitatis Redintegratio*, all promulgated by Pope Paul VI on 21st November, 1964. "These Eastern Churches share equal dignity, so that none of them is superior to the others as regards rite ... under the guidance of the Roman Pontiff" (*Orientalium Ecclesiarum*).

father and of the inexplicable restoration of life to the dead including himself. It is understandable that the oppressed people who followed his teachings rejoiced, "The Lord God is amongst us!"

Jesus Christ's followers, congregated as Christians, were persecuted by authority, as was their inspirational Son of God founder, and crystallised to solidity as the Catholic Church. The Catholic Church in union with its theological equivalents as it evolved came to be the only Christian Church in this world. Inspired by the assurances of the founder, Jesus Christ, the embodiment of the Creator God on Earth, that he would be with them "all days, even to the consummation of the world", the Catholic Church formalised the ongoing presence of God in this world in those rituals which it believes are enacted by God through the ministry of his ordained priesthood. Such rituals are known as sacraments, the outward sign of God's presence in this world. Sacramentality is the fact of Catholicism and an essential foundation for a full and informed appreciation of Catholic teaching, something that is sadly lacking in many public commentators, critics of the Church and increasing numbers of post-Vatican II Catholics, including some clergy, members of religious orders and the proponents of renewal or reform.

The seven sacraments of the Catholic Church are Baptism (the formal sanctification of a human life), Confirmation (the confirmation of commitment to full union with God within the Catholic Church), Reconciliation (confession and forgiveness of sin, formerly known as Penance), Eucharist (the consecration of bread and wine in the Mass), *Holy Orders* (ordination to priesthood), Matrimony (marriage) and The Anointing of the Sick (the anointing with holy oils and forgiveness of sin in the sick or dying, formerly known as Extreme Unction and the Last Rites of the Catholic Church). The presence of God, not only amongst humankind, but integrally as part of the human being itself through the sacraments, is the signature of this sacramental Church. In this integration resides the Catholic appreciation of what constitutes human life and what it means in the living of daily life. The on-going presence of God as the risen Christ in humankind determines the Catholic Church's teachings and moral tenets across the vast panorama of human activity. To understand Catholicism is to understand the sacraments.

Sacraments are the immutable difference between Catholicism and Protestantism. Protestantism has its origins from Catholicism principally in the personages of Martin Luther, a Catholic priest driven by personal preferences, disagreement with some aspects of Catholic practice and a differing interpretation of the requirements for salvation. Luther was followed soon after by King Henry VIII, a Catholic English king whose procreative activities fell outside the moral tenets of the Catholic Church and placed him in conflict with papal authority. Failure to achieve resolution of the disagreements between the king and the papacy lead to the reformation of the Catholic Church in England according to the king's requirements and not those of the Church founded by Christ himself. The English Reformation in real terms represents an estrangement from Catholic recognition of the presence of God amongst humanity in that the reforms of Henry VIII and his Catholic henchmen, Archbishop Cranmer and Cardinal Wolsey, abandoned the sacraments. The definitive text prepared by Cranmer, the *Second Book of Prayer,* which is essentially the basis of the prayer book used in the Anglican Church[3] to the present day, was imposed on English Catholicism by the *Second Act of Uniformity* of 1552 [4] Only the sacraments of baptism and marriage were retained, the former because baptism was a major centre piece of Luther's European continental Protestantism on which Cranmer relied for support in his dismantling of Catholic England, and the

---

[3] The Anglican Church (Church of England) is essentially the same as the Episcopal Church in the USA.

[4] Ref: Culkin, G. *The English Reformation.* Paternoster Publications, London, 1954: 51-55.

latter, because both Cranmer and Wolsey, avowed Catholic celibate priests, were promised permission to marry their illicit mistresses in the king's new English Church in return for their support in his "great matter", namely his dispute with the papacy over his immoral behaviours which embraced murder, adultery and dissolution of his sacramental marriage without genuine cause

The abandonment of sacramental Catholicism in the establishment of Protestantism essentially means that within Protestantism there is no genuine celebration of Christian Eucharist as understood in Catholicism, no forgiveness of sin through Reconciliation or through the Anointing of the Sick, and no genuine ordination to the priesthood as instituted by Christ through Holy Orders. Perhaps the nature of the sacramental Catholic Church and its difference from Protestantism is best understood by comparison of the Catholic Mass with the Anglican Divine Service. The Catholic Mass is the central essence of Catholicism and, indeed, Christianity. It is the celebration of the Sacrament of Eucharist.

Catholic teaching and belief is that as a sacrament is the external sign of God in our midst, that God, albeit in spiritual form, is truly present through the ministry of his priest which sanctifies or consecrates the commemorative gifts of bread and wine described by Jesus Christ at the last supper before his death as his body and blood, his very essence. At that supper according to the available written record, Christ commissioned his apostles (ordained them to priesthood in Catholic teaching) to sanctify offerings of bread and wine in his memory, not once or twice, but for all time. Catholicism teaches that these consecrated gifts do embody the true essence of the risen Christ as one with the Father and the Holy Spirit in the Blessed Trinity, three persons in one God, the Real Presence. The process of change in essence of simple bread and wine is called transubstantiation. And therein lies the major stumbling block on the road to reconciliation of Protestantism with Catholicism and its equivalents and also the basis of the much criticised claim by the Catholic Church that it represents the one true, universal, apostolic, Christian Church.

While some Protestant Churches, notably within Anglicanism, have in recent times resurrected a service based on the Catholic Mass (even to the point of proclaiming that the Catholic Mass is very similar to the Anglican service), that segment of the Anglican service which emulates the Catholic consecration of bread and wine is considered in Protestantism as symbolic, not sacramental, and not associated with transubstantiation of the bread and wine.[5] It is clear that a yawning chasm exists between Catholic Christianity and Protestant Christianity. That dividing chasm was created by the abandonment of the presence of God embodied in a sacramental life and represents a far greater schism than the well documented schism between Antioch and Rome in that the Church in Antioch retained the sacramental nature of its practice. The post-Vatican II proponents for renewal and reform are wandering in the footsteps of Martin Luther and Henry VIII, failing to recognise the sacramentality of the Church instituted by Christ. Such diversion has serious implications for Catholicism in the questioning of the truth of scripture and tradition, particularly in matters of Christ's delegation of authority for his Church on Earth to his apostles, embodied in our world in the papacy.

Human life then, in Catholic teaching, cannot be divorced from God amongst us, from a sacramental presence, from a spiritual component, the soul, from the soul's destiny, eternal life in the bosom of its creator, any more than it can be divorced from the all embracing human society in which it exists. It is only when human life and the world are seen in these terms that Catholic teaching can be easily understood and is perhaps the reason why it is widely perceived as

---

5 Within Lutheranism, Eucharist is considered to be sacramental and the concept of the real presence in the consecrated bread and wine is not regarded as simply symbolic.

interfering in the lives of today's men and women. Perhaps the Church is not interfering. Rather, it is simply accepting the responsibility for the stewardship of all creation, all creatures great and small and the environment in which we live, a commission which the Catholic Church believes comes from God the Creator. If indeed the Church is God's chosen steward of all creation, the basis of its authority in prescribing the requirements of that stewardship is clearly pivotal to the acceptance of that authority.

4
CHURCH AUTHORITY

*Wherever there is a man who exercises authority,
there is a man who resists authority*

Oscar Wilde, *De Profundis*

An anti-democratic killjoy

The modern day would-be reformers and renewalists frequently disregard, disrespect and reject papal authority and seek a redefinition of moral law to suit their personal needs and beliefs – shades of the seeds of the English Reformation of King Henry VIII. Since the Second Vatican Council the teaching authority of the Church in matters of faith and morals under the Christ-given guidance of the papacy finds itself under attack by reformers clamouring for a hybrid style of people's democracy under the umbrella of their interpretations of collegiality and church. These reformers, in their quest for the emasculation of papal authority, continue to bring inestimable and unnecessary damage to the Church, despite claims to be acting in accordance with the reforms of Vatican II, inspired by "the spirit". Saint Ignatius Loyola might caution that not all spirit is necessarily good, derived from God.

One of the distinguishing characteristics of Catholicism[6] is the existence of a central guiding authority dispensing a code of moral behaviour which accords with the scholarly interpretation of sacred

---

[6] Catholicism or the Catholic Church used in this text will imply inclusion of the equivalent Eastern Catholic Churches in full communion with Catholicism under the authority of the Roman Pontiff and excludes all Protestantism including those Anglican and Episcopalian Churches which consider themselves Catholic yet are outside the teaching authority of the Catholic Church.

scripture and tradition. Such authoritarianism has always been contrary to the Australian rebellious character born out of its convict origins, the famous battles for rights at Eureka Stockade in Victoria and Vinegar Hill in New South Wales, the secular sainthood of Edward (Ned) Kelly, the gamest and most famous outlaw of all and the elevation of the World War I heroes, the Anzacs, to a religious significance in their voluntary sacrifice of individual human life for others. There are many references to authority in both the Old and New Testaments, too numerous to be elaborated upon here and beyond the scope and intent of this work. In the gospels, however, there are very clear directives recorded, through which Christ bestowed responsibility and authority for the ongoing direction of his Church on those whom he had chosen as his priests, the apostles under the leadership of Peter.[7] The interpretations of scripture and tradition by the Magisterium (the teaching authority of the Church) are often derived after many years of consideration and the canvassing of advice from learned counsel consisting of students of scripture and tradition, persons of expertise in a particular field of human endeavour such as medicine or the

---

7 Matt. 18:18 (16-19): "And so I tell all of you: what you prohibit on earth will be prohibited in heaven, and what you permit on earth will be permitted in heaven. And I tell you more: whenever two of you on earth agree about anything you pray for, it will be done for you by my father in heaven. For where two or three come together in my name, I am there with them."

Matt. 28:19-20: Jesus drew near and said to them, "I have been given all authority in heaven and on earth. Go then to all peoples everywhere and make them my disciples: baptise them in the name of the Father, the Son, and the Holy Spirit, and teach them to obey everything I have commanded you. And I will be with you always, to the end of the age."

Luke. 22:19: Then he took a piece of bread, gave thanks to God, broke it, and gave it to them, saying, "This is my body which is given for you. Do this in memory of me."

John. 20:21-23: Jesus said to them again, "Peace be with you. As the Father sent me I also send you." Then he breathed on them and said, "Receive the Holy Spirit. If you forgive people's sins, they are forgiven; if you do not forgive them, they are not forgiven."

law and lay persons of many denominations and life experiences. The teaching authority of the Church is responsible for applying the interpretations arising from its determinations of the morality or otherwise of a particular human or societal activity to the living of day to day human life.

This mechanism is fundamentally different from the moral considerations of many non-Catholic denominations of Christianity where such a structure has been abandoned in favour of largely personal interpretations of the Bible dependent on the literal word, and in others to limited authority vested in local communities and civil law which fail to embrace a comprehensive morality across all endeavours in the living of day to day life. For example, quite apart from sacred scripture, the *Catechism of the Catholic Church* contains no fewer than 2865 tenets of moral/doctrinal teaching compared with, say, the 39 *Articles of Religion* in the Anglican Church, the 13 *Articles of Faith* in the Mormon Church or the exclusive authority of the Bible alone as embraced by many protestant and evangelical denominations and some quasi-Christian sects. Since its inception over 2,000 years ago, Catholicism has continued to address all aspects of human life and embody these in its moral teachings determined by a number of Church councils, apostolic constitutions and papal encyclicals.

In their demands for a greater place for the laity in the determinations of the moral teachings of the Church, modern day reformers appeal to the Vatican II call for collegiality, to the definition of Church as all members of the body of believers, laity and ordained priesthood, joined in a democratisation of the Church through authority vested in the people in apostolate with a local diocesan bishop not subject to obedience to the supreme moral authority of the papacy. It is necessary to pay heed to these opinions and examine their validity or otherwise since their continuing presence in the post-conciliar Church causes so much dissent, confusion and unnecessary damage. Collegiality is a complex word for tribalism, for any coming together of a group of persons under a common binding philosophy or practice. Since its very inception, the Catholic Church has been collegiate, constituted as an organised body of persons with shared functions and privileges but under the guiding authority of Christ and, through his own Word, exercised in this world by his ordained priesthood with the Pope as the supreme authority to which all other authority is subservient. In Catholicism, moral authority rests ultimately with the Pope in his role as the Christ-delegated authority representing the God Creator in the human world.

To embrace the collegiality of the Catholic Church requires a belief that Jesus, the risen Lord, was indeed God himself, one with the God Creator and with the Holy Spirit, the all pervasive spirit or presence of God in this world. This triumvirate[8], the Holy Trinity, is one of Catholicism's defining signatures. Belonging means acceptance, not only of belief in this God, but also of the moral authority and trust in God's delegation of that authority to his ordained priesthood as described in sacred scripture, qualified by the concept of the supreme authority of the Pope, the successor to Christ's chosen shepherd, Peter.[9] It is this that has come under challenge in the modern Church and which would seem to reflect a lack of belief, humility and trust in God. A hybrid form of authority based on secular democracy and a collegiality wherein the people can determine, manipulate, dispel, alter or terminate a college teaching or format of practice through a lobby group is indeed a most anti-collegiate prescription and a system resembling much of non-catholic Christianity. Such is what some present day reformers seek.

Collegiality is addressed in *Lumen Gentium* (The Dogmatic

---

8 Triumvirate = set of any three persons in authority.
9 Matt. 16:18-19: "And so I tell you, Peter: you are a rock, and on this rock foundation I will build my church, and not even death will ever be able to overcome it. I will give you the keys of the Kingdom of heaven; what you prohibit on earth will be prohibited in heaven, and what you permit on earth will be permitted in heaven."

Constitution of the Church), the third of the Vatican II documents, promulgated by Pope Paul VI on 21 November 1964. This document was passed by 2,151 votes to 5 by the delegates after many modifications when the earlier drafts appeared to remove supreme authority from the Pope and bestow greater authority for faith and morals on the bishops. Such a radical change had the potential to dissolve universal collegiality in the Church through licensing local dioceses in a practice and theology arrived at by a local bishop and his lay apostolate without papal approval. Such a prescription has the potential to emasculate the universal teachings of Catholicism. This was witnessed in Queensland in recent times in the defiance of papal authority by a diocesan bishop in a matter of Church teaching and in the archdiocese of Brisbane by a diocesan priest's hybrid celebration of Mass well beyond the sacred nature of the Mass and the Vatican II changes in liturgy. If such actions were permitted throughout the Church, Catholicism could become a divided conglomeration of personalised local Church communities without the universality of one identifying ideology and theology. Such a possibility was recognised by the Council and was, therefore, specifically written out of *Lumen Gentium* in an explanatory addendum.

Collegiality and authority in the Church are explained in *Lumen Gentium* and elaborated on as follows in a direct quote from the addendum:[10]

> 3. The College, which does not exist without its head, is said 'to exist also as the subject of supreme and full power in the universal Church'. This must be admitted of necessity so that *the fullness of power belongs to the Roman Pontiff and is not called into question.* For the College, always and of necessity, includes its head, because in the college he preserves unhindered his function as Christ's Vicar and as Pastor of the universal

---

10 Highlighting in this quote is that of the author and not a feature of the original document.

Church. In other words, it is not a distinction between the Roman Pontiff and the bishops taken collectively, but a distinction between the Roman Pontiff taken separately and the Roman Pontiff together with the bishops. *Since the Supreme Pontiff is head of the College, he alone is able to perform certain actions which are not at all within the competence of the bishops*, e.g., convoking the College and directing it, approving norms of action etc. Cf. Modus 81. *It is up to the judgement of the Supreme Pontiff, to whose care Christ's whole flock has been entrusted, to determine according to the needs of the Church as they change over the course of centuries, the way in which this care may best be exercised – whether in a personal or a collegial way. The Roman Pontiff, taking account of the Church's welfare proceeds according to his own discretion in arranging, promoting and approving the exercise of collegial activity.*

4. As Supreme Pastor of the Church, the Supreme Pontiff can always exercise his power at will, as his very office demands. Though it is always in existence, the College is not as a result permanently engaged in strictly collegial activity; the Church's Tradition makes this clear. *In other words, the College is not always 'fully active'; rather, it acts as a college in the strict sense only from time to time and only with the consent of its head.* The phrase *'with the consent of its head' is used to avoid the idea of dependence on some kind of outsider;* the term 'consent' suggests rather communion between the head and the members, and implies the need for an act which belongs properly to the competence of the head. This is explicitly affirmed in n.22, 12, and is explained at the end of that section. The word 'only' takes in all cases. It is evident from this that the norms approved by the supreme authority must always be observed. Cf. Modus 84.

It is clear throughout that it is a question of the bishops acting in conjunction with their head, never of the bishops acting independently of the Pope. In the latter instance, without the action of the head, the bishops are not able to act as a College: this is clear from the concept of "College". This hierarchical communion of all with the Supreme Pontiff is certainly firmly established in tradition.

Such is authority as defined by Vatican II, remote from the clamourings of the modern day reformers including some bishops, priests and laity.

Vatican II did not, therefore, in the light of *Lumen Gentium,* embrace a form of collegiality which excludes the pope as supreme authority over the remainder of the priesthood or bestows any authority whatever on the laity. The true spirit of Vatican II, a good thing, has affirmed the authority of the Church as currently constituted and that spirit does not reside in the hostile environment created by some reformers, those bishops, priests and laity who, "in the name and spirit of Vatican II", continue to damage the Church through their brazen disregard and disrespect for papal authority. Their adopted position is clearly not supported by Vatican II. It is time to keep their own counsel, stop their damaging, public carping against the Church they profess to love, or alternatively, to embrace outside Catholicism the particular form of Protestantism they seek.

5

Ecumenism

... that they may all be one

John 17: 20-21

One apostolic Church

Since the Second Vatican Council, renewal and reform of the Church has already come to pass through the true spirit of Vatican II. This is perhaps most evidenced by the ecumenical movement within Catholicism. Before Vatican II, Australia was a society divided by sectarian tribalism in what might be described as a religious cold war which dissolved in matters of hot war. In war between nations and in sporting contests, Australia versus the rest, the tribes became one, mates in a temporary secular tribe identifiable only as Australian. War and sport are Australia's great levellers and assimilators. Going to war or playing sport for Australia transcends all politics, religious adherence and race. Catholics, Protestants, Jews, Muslims, Hindus, Buddhists, atheists and agnostics regardless of racial origin become one – all "Aussies".[11]

Sectarianism in Australia was predicated mainly on the distrust between the two major population groups, the working class Irish Catholics and the conservative British Protestants. Britain, the authority that governed Australia, had the inglorious history of

---

11 There was a time, however, when it was extremely difficult indeed for a Catholic to be selected to represent Australia in the quintessentially British game of cricket, Australia's national game, and when both Catholics and Jews were excluded from membership of some of Australia's most prestigious clubs, associations and political party selections for representative government in one of the world's founding democracies.

ongoing religious oppression of Catholic Ireland and bigotry towards Catholics, a bigotry enshrined in its civil laws regulating succession to the throne and the administration of the Anglican Church. In the experiences of Eureka stockade and the Vinegar Hill rebellions, both led by Irish rebels, the plethora of Irish Catholic bushrangers in the country's history, the armed rebellions of the 1916 Easter Uprising in Dublin and the continuing armed rebellion of the IRA against British rule in Northern Ireland, Australian conservatism in its British origins saw Irish Catholics as potential armed rebels. Catholics in Australia, an unashamed braggart amongst the modern democracies, were excluded from conservative political participation as federal parliamentarians until the mid-1970s. Many were denied engagement by Protestant employers. For Catholics, community with Protestantism was itself a form of rebellion against Catholicism. Political affiliations were essentially anti-Protestant toryism, expressed in widespread adherence to the left wing Labor Party amongst Catholics. Paradoxically perhaps, the Catholic Church under the guidance of Archbishop Daniel Mannix in Melbourne defeated the Labor prime minister, Billy Hughes, in two referendums calling for conscription of Australians to the British forces in World War I despite the fact that many Catholics voluntarily served. Indeed, the largest recruitment from schools in Australia came from two of the largest Catholic colleges, St Ignatius, Riverview, in Sydney, and St Josephs, Nudgee, in Brisbane.

Catholics themselves could not attend a church service, baptism, wedding or funeral in a Protestant church and could not marry a Protestant in a Catholic church, essentially because of Protestantism's abandonment of the Presence of Christ in its non-sacramental rituals, the very antithesis of Catholicism. The "mixed marriage" was frowned upon and caused much heartache for pre-Vatican II Catholics who happened to find a Protestant soul mate and equally for those Protestants who found the same in a Catholic. Children of both sides were exiled from home, some were disinherited and family relationships were broken because of a proposed Catholic-Protestant marriage. For Catholics and Christianity generally, the Jews were responsible for the death of Christ, seen as a bad thing, even though Christianity deemed Christ's death was God's intention for the salvation of humankind, perceived as the fulfilment of prophecy and the best thing that could ever have happened for the human race. Indeed, the death of Christ was central to Christianity itself. Non-Christian religions were pagan and meaningless. The positions taken by the protagonists in such sectarian nonsense meant societal conflict and unnecessary, distinctly un-Christian, mutual alienation.

The movement towards Christian unity of the thousands[12] of denominations claiming Christianity has been addressed in *Unitatis Redintegratio* (The Decree on Ecumenism, Second Vatican Council, 21 November 1964). The implementation of the spirit of this document represents perhaps the greatest reform or renewal of Catholicism arising from Vatican II, not only as a great liberator for Australian Catholicism but also as an achievement for society at large. The introduction to this document states:

> The restoration of unity among all Christians is one of the principal concerns of the Second Vatican Council. Christ the Lord founded one Church and one Church only. However, many Christian communions present themselves to men as the true inheritors of Jesus Christ; all indeed profess to be followers of the Lord but differ in mind and go their different ways, as if Christ Himself were divided.

Vatican II thus reaffirmed the Christian history that the Catholic Church had its origins with Jesus of Nazareth and maintains an unbroken link with its origins to the present day, the basis of its much criticised claim that it is the one, true, universal, apostolic Christian Church, a claim that continues to stoke the fires of sectarianism in some quarters.

---

12 Wikipedia records 41,000 Christian denominations.

While the Council did not resile from any of the Church's claims regarding its exclusive authenticity, it did affirm that Christianity was not the exclusive preserve of the Catholic Church. Rather, *Unitatis Redintegratio* recognises quite clearly that Christianity exists where any people are gathered together in the name of Jesus the Christ.[13] Further, the document also states clearly that the Catholic Church's stance is that all Christianity becomes one in Christ, in the one apostolic Church, meaning the Catholic Church, under the authority of St Peter's successor, the Pope, as commissioned by Christ,[14] (*Unitatis Redintegratio,* Ch I, 2) with its established doctrine, not doctrine modified to accommodate various human personal preferences nor to couch favour in the modern secular world. Again in *Unitatis Redintegratio* (Ch I, 3), the Council acknowledged that from the beginnings of the Catholic Church "... quite large communities came to be separated from full communion with the Catholic Church – for which, often enough, men of both sides were to blame". Acknowledging that the descendants of those breakaway groups are blameless, the Council stated that "it remains true that all who have been justified by faith in Baptism are members of Christ's body [the Church], and have a right to be called Christian, and so are correctly accepted as brothers by the children of the Catholic Church".

The shortest of the Vatican II documents, *Nostra Aetate* (Declaration on the Relation of the Church to Non-Christian Religions, Pope Paul VI, 28 October 1965), states in its opening, "... the Church ... in her task of promoting unity and love among men, indeed among nations ... considers above all in this declaration what men have in common

---

13 Matt. 18:19-20: "And I tell you more: whenever two of you on earth agree about anything you pray for, it will be done for you by my Father in heaven. For where two or three come together in my name, I am there with them."

14 John 17:20-21: "I pray not only for them [his disciples], but also for those who believe in me because of this message. I pray that they may all be one. Father! May they be in me, just as you are in me and I am in you. May they be one, so that the world will believe that you sent me."

and what draws them to fellowship". This document also recognises the existence in all men of an innate knowledge and appreciation of human virtue, the natural law, expressed in different ways by non-Christian religions like Hinduism and Buddhism and states:

> The Catholic Church rejects nothing that is true and holy in these religions. She regards with sincere reverence those ways of conduct and of life, those precepts and teachings which, though differing in many aspects from the ones she holds and sets forth, nonetheless often reflect a ray of that Truth which enlightens all men. [The natural law]

However, in recognising and saying that, Vatican II "... proclaims, and ever must proclaim Christ, the way, the truth, and the life,[15] in whom men may find the fullness of religious life, in whom God has reconciled all things to Himself".

In section 3 of *Nostra Aetate*, Vatican II expressed its esteem for Islam in its adherence to one God and its valuing of the moral life and worship of God especially through prayer, almsgiving and fasting. In this section also, the spiritual patrimony common to Christians and Jews is recognised and the pre-Vatican II perception that the Jews as a people are responsible for the death of Christ is definitively rejected. The place of the Jews in Catholicism is made clear in the following statement:

> Furthermore, in her [the Catholic Church] rejection of every persecution against any man [human being], the Church, mindful of the patrimony she shares with the Jews and moved not by political reasons but by the Gospel's spiritual love, decries hatred, persecutions, displays of anti-Semitism, directed against Jews at any time and by anyone.

Again, in its final section (5), *Nostra Aetate*, concludes:

---

15 John 14:6: "I am the way, the truth and the life; no-one goes to the Father except by me."

> The Church reproves, as foreign to the mind of Christ, any discrimination against men or harassment of them because of their race, colour, condition of life [poverty or riches] or religion. On the contrary, following in the footsteps of the holy Apostles Peter and Paul, this sacred synod ardently implores the Christian faithful to maintain good fellowship among the nations[16] and, if possible, to live for their part in peace with all men, so that they may truly be sons [and daughters] of the father who is in heaven.

Genuine ecumenism is thus one of the great achievements of Vatican II. In Australia, sectarianism with its societal and personal damage has largely dissipated. Distrust of each other in the mainstream Christian religions seemingly no longer exists and religion is no longer the great divisor that it once was, although pockets of anti-Catholicism still exist in some Protestant denominations. Catholics generally now see all people of Christian adherence as genuine people of God and do not see Catholicism as having the exclusive rights to salvation and all that is Christian. After a millennium of schism, the Eastern rite sacramental Churches and Catholicism have grown closer on the road to reunion. So too, the Anglican Church has progressed rapidly towards some form of reconciliation with Catholicism, not at an official level yet but in the increasing conversion of Anglican clergy and people to Catholicism with accompanying ordination of Anglican clergymen (not clergywomen) to the Catholic priesthood. In a Joint Declaration in 1999, agreement was reached between the Lutheran World Federation and the Catholic Church on the Doctrine of Justification, the basis of Luther's founding protest which gave birth to Protestantism. The protest is over. The foundation stone of Protestantism is no more.

---

16 1 Peter 2:12: "Your conduct among the heathen should be so good that when they accuse you of being evildoers, they will have to recognise your good deeds and so praise God on the day of his coming."

Recognition by the Catholic Church of genuine Christianity in many non-Catholic communions has led to embrace of the Catholic Church by ministers of other Christian religions and the establishment of ordinariates wherein these ministers can be formally ordained as priests in the Catholic Church. This represents a practical outcome of the spirit of Christian unity and has been one of the great outcomes of Vatican II. Some of these ministers, now ordained Catholic priests, are married with families. That the Catholic Church now espouses both celibate and married priests, this outcome of ecumenism may well herald the coming of the acceptance of marriage in the priesthood generally, something which would remove what is almost certainly a deterrent for many good men to enter the priesthood in the modern world.

In simple terms, then, ecumenism as urged by Vatican II does not imply that the Catholic Church changes or abandons certain doctrines to become one with other religions but rather, that other religions become one with Catholicism, the one, true, apostolic Church instituted by Christ. That process is well underway in the modern Church, not by coercion but through consultation and understanding with the revelation that comes from that. In the Vatican II vision, all Christianity is to be reconciled with its origins and all non-Christian religions are to be respected for their recognition of a supreme being (God) through the innate understanding in all men and women of the moral values inherent in the natural law.

Since Vatican II, particularly in the papacies of John Paul II and Benedict XVI, both of whom were inspired by Pope John XXIII's great rapport with the Jewish people (he was responsible together with Pope Pius XII for the survival of hundreds of thousands of Jewish people during Hitler's genocide), great progress has been made in the relations between Catholicism and Judaism. Christianity owes much to Judaism in that it was born from the ancient Jewish belief in one God and a code of ethics based on the natural law. These religions have so much in common that the dialogue that now exists between them can only improve both to the greater glory of God, in keeping with their very purpose. It was fundamental that Vatican II recognised that Christ was a Jewish man and that it was not the Jewish religion that was responsible for his death by crucifixion. Finally, the recognition of goodness in Islam expressed in its monotheism and practices of fasting and almsgiving can only be helpful and more likely than criticism to dispel conflict. It is hoped that Islam responds to the genuine intent of this recognition as a unifying influence.

Such is the Catholic stance on ecumenism – "... that they may all be one". In this vision there is no place for the abandonment of established doctrine or moral precepts simply to meet the desire for Christian unity or to accommodate modern lifestyles and tastes as stated by Pope John XXIII when he convened the Second Vatican Council and reiterated in *Unitatis Redintegratio* (Ch II, 11): "Nothing is so foreign to the spirit of ecumenism as a false irenicism [peace accord] in which the purity of Catholic doctrine suffers loss and its genuine and certain meaning is clouded."

While the post-conciliar ecumenism is a good thing, unfortunately, misinterpretations of the intent of Vatican II, that they may all be one, by some clergy and lay exponents of unity have been bad and damaging to true Christianity through the abandonment of scriptural and traditional Christian teaching in favour of human socialisation in an inclusive society, rather than in an authentic and inclusive Church, defined as the sacramental Church instituted by Christ, not by men. In the present day, that Church is the Catholic Church and its Eastern sacramental equivalents. The ecumenical movement in the Catholic Church in some quarters, like so many other aspects of the post-Vatican II Church, has been hijacked by Catholic dissidents with essentially a Protestant agenda which serves "dialogue, education and mutual respect", the great liberators from responsibility and definitive action in the modern world.

6
Liturgy

Ad majorem Dei gloriam
The Jesuit motto

To the greater glory of God

Not all reforms and renewals after Vatican II served the Church well. The change in the liturgy of the Mass detailed in *Sacrosanctum Consilium* (Constitution on the Sacred Liturgy, Pope Paul VI, 4 December 1963), was potentially the greatest innovation of the Council for the Catholic laity. All changes in the liturgy required approval by the local diocesan bishops under the authority of the papacy. Further, liturgical changes were envisaged by the Council as facilitators of greater lay participation in the sacramental life of the Church and, indeed, to bring the laity to a form of participating ministry, something exclusive to the priesthood in the pre-Vatican II Church.

In the Catholic Church, the liturgy embodies not only the celebrated rituals but also the compendium of reverence, prayer, sacred music, church architecture and art, all conspiring towards the elevation of the human spirit towards God, alive and risen amongst his people in the Sacraments. The liturgical changes that came after Vatican II promised a renewed and inclusive Church but the reality fell far short of the ideal and indeed inflicted more than a little damage on the very laity for whom the changes were intended and on the priesthood itself, both of these conspiring towards a loss of Catholic identity in society at large.

The priest joining rather than leading the laity in the celebration of the Mass in a common language brought a sense of community, of belonging, of family and of unity with the priesthood. The very architecture of a Catholic Church changed from the heaven bound loftiness of towering arches pointing the way towards God in his heaven to a more inclusive structure with the altar being central, like the table in a dining room accessible by all, rather than the stepping stone between the priest and God in his heaven with the laity as seemingly uninvited onlookers. The sanctuary, the Holy of Holies,[17] where the priest celebrated the Sacrament of Eucharist separated from the laity by the often elaborately decorated altar rail where the laity knelt to receive the consecrated host in communion, was replaced by a sanctuary opened to the people. The people were invited into the Holy of Holies. The pre-Vatican II celebratory priest at God's sacrificial altar, with his back to the people and his arms extended upwards towards heaven in prayer, now faced the people so that his arms, outstretched, embraced them. This was a seemingly more inclusive Church.

In the pre-Vatican II Church, the priest alone prayed before his procession to the sanctuary to celebrate the Eucharist, "Introibo ad altari dei" ("I will enter unto the altar of God"). This was replaced by the Entrance Antiphon, either a prayer or hymn of praise to God, sung by all in company with the celebrating priest, not in Latin but in the vernacular. The people joined with the priest in procession to the sanctuary to lead the prayer and scriptural readings in the introductory part of the Mass, the Liturgy of the Word, previously the exclusive province of the ordained priest. Through the introduction

---

[17] The room known as the Holy of Holies was the innermost and most sacred area of the ancient tabernacle of Moses and the temple of Jerusalem, accessible only to the high priest. It contained the symbol of Israel's special relationship with God, the Ark of the Covenant. In the Catholic Church, the sanctuary contained in the tabernacle the consecrated host of unleavened bread, representing the embodiment of God on earth and, like the Holy of Holies, a place inhabited only by the sacred and excluding the profane.

of the vernacular in place of Latin the laity was admitted to a form of ministry of the liturgy. This also meant that both the spoken and the sung liturgy were more meaningful to those who did not have a knowledge or written translation of the Latin and promised greater understanding of the rituals (sacraments), particularly for the young. All of these changes suited the Australian psyche. We were all mates now, not just spectators at a ritual incanted in a foreign language. The laity now entered unto the altar of God.

Involvement of the laity was also realised in the development of parish pastoral councils, arising from the organisational remodelling of diocesan administration according to *Christus Dominus* (The Decree Concerning the Pastoral Office of Bishops in the Church, Pope Paul VI, 28 October 1965). Parish pastoral councils were constituted to act as advisory bodies of lay persons chosen because of particular expertise in various aspects of day to day secular life. These councils helped the priest in his administration of the local parish, served an advisory role in matters not within the priest's expertise and provided additional roles in the everyday running of some ministries serving the parish community. The parish council, however, is not an autonomous authority, such authority belonging to the priest alone, modified by his subsidiary role to the authority of the bishop and ultimately, the pope. Such councils are thus another form of collegiality in the post-Vatican II conversation. It was to be expected perhaps that such a system could be hijacked by a particular vested interest or clique within the laity and thus fail in its purpose and cause more disruption than help in the parish. And such did happen and continues to happen in some parish councils infiltrated by reformers and restorationists both, pursuing either personal or group agendas in the name of the spirit of Vatican II and in a self-absorption lacking the humility that characterised their Christ.

All action produces a reaction. Reaction, however, can be either good or bad. Some changes after Vatican II were good and long overdue. However, this great good brought some bad, not intended by the Council and human rather than divine in its origins. Not all of the liturgical changes were in accord with the determinations of the Council but arose from personal interpretations of the Vatican II documents and attempts by various individuals to implement local changes according to their preference. One such piece of implementation, for example, was the replacement of the crucifix behind the altar by a projected photograph of a surfer with his board under his arm peering out to sea into a brilliantly coloured dawn. The image resembled a cross formed by the horizontal surf board and the vertical surfer. The symbolism might have been that in the local church, a community situated on a famous Australian surfing beach, Christ was to be found not as a sacrificial lamb but in the inane spirituality and exhilaration of catching the perfect wave, "my own, personal spirituality".

In another parish with a social justice, pro-Aboriginal mission, a dying scrub turkey with wings outstretched replaced the crucified Christ dying on the cross. The symbolism might have been that the Australian Aboriginal people, exclusive like the scrub turkey to Australia, were the crucified, not the Christ. Both of these liturgical interpretations of the spirit of Vatican II were local products undertaken without the authority of the bishop or the papacy in flagrant disregard for the Vatican II teachings on authority. Liturgical licence, that some believed was the intent of the Council, plagued the post-conciliar Church and has done enormous damage. While the laity may have been elevated towards priesthood in the post-conciliar Church, many priests stepped down to become part of the laity in a "more relevant human Church", similar in their opinion to the early Church of the oppressed society into which Jesus of Nazareth was born.

The Second Vatican Council in truth set out to bring the Church to greater relevance in the world of today, a very different society from the undeveloped world of the Middle East at the time when Christ and his followers lived. The priesthood in the pre-Vatican II Church was a highly respected and revered occupation, not only within Catholicism but in many Christian denominations. Such respect applied across denominations in the public perception despite their theological divisions. Ministers of religion were respected in Australian society regardless of denomination.

In the wake of Vatican II, however, numerous Catholic priests abandoned any identifying dress, presumably ashamed or embarrassed to be publicly identified as a priest, or alternatively, to allow them to partake unrecognised in the new society. Many were no longer "Father" and became at their insistence "Bill", "Fred" or "Jack". The priesthood fell victim to this new liberation with a great acceleration of priests abandoning the ministry in the decades after Vatican II. Sadly, the scandalous sexual abuse by some priests of both adults and children, greatly accelerated in the decades following Vatican II in parallel with the secular sexual revolution throughout the Western world, has brought the Church to its knees.. The mysticism of the priesthood was quietly eroded and, with this, the role model that had probably inspired the priest himself to take Holy Orders no longer existed in an easily identifiable way in the modern era. Many Australian seminaries, full at the time of Vatican II, no longer exist and the few that are still operative have very few students. The call to priesthood, becoming rarer in today's Western society, might be better heard if those liberated priests of today were to resume a life that shone as a role model to the young rather than a life that is mundanely human, perhaps too like ordinary men, and thus undifferentiated from society at large.[18]

Latin, the exclusive language of the Catholic Mass before Vatican II, was not a language of day to day communication in any society. While the introduction of the local vernacular in place of the Latin

---

18 The Irish inquiry into sexual abuse by Catholic priests in the Dublin Archdiocese analysed the total number of complaints received from the 1940s up until 2009 and unveiled an accelerating increase in the number of complaints per decade from 2% (% of total number of complaints) in the 1940s to 9% in the 1950s and steadily increasing up to 38% during the 1960s, 70s and 80s. From 1990 to 2010 the percentage of total complaints has fallen to 2% across the 2000s. (The percentages refer to the number of complaints made per decade, not to the percentage of priests in the Archdiocese). A Vatican delegation appearing before a hearing of the United Nations Committee on the Rights of Children, held in Geneva on 16 January 2014, said that the Vatican continues to receive around 600 complaints against abusive priests from around the world every year, many dating back to the 1960s, 70s and 80s, the post Vatican II period corresponding with the great acceleration in abuse revealed by the findings in the Irish inquiry. This confluence of Vatican II with the acceleration of sexual abuse in parallel with the same in secular society at large does not indicate that Vatican II is the cause – such a deduction represents the logical fallacy of *post hoc ergo propter hoc* (after this, therefore because of this). It is far more logical to expect that the increase in abuse came as a result of the sexual revolution and relative secularisation of the priesthood (making it "more human" and bringing it down from its erstwhile pedestal) combined perhaps with the failure of Vatican II to liberalise celibacy in the priesthood. In other words, a failure in personal morality in the abusing priests themselves. That does not excuse, however, the way in which the Vatican and local dioceses managed the matter during those decades ('60s, '70s and '80s). In Australia, enquiries into institutional sexual abuse are still in process and statistics on the extent of this problem are not yet available. It is the fact, however, that as far as the Catholic Church is concerned the problem as a current issue is far less than it was in the decades mentioned above and the enquiries have revealed that the Catholic Church is not alone and that the problem seems to be systemic across all aspects of secular modern society and across all religious denominations – all victims of the sexual revolution and the abandonment of a moral life. For its part, the Catholic Church in Australia under Cardinal George Pell established the first response in the world to help victims of the sexual revolution, a response which was exported to other countries by request, but which although imperfect in some aspects and since improved upon, has earned no credit.

was seen to be a great vehicle for the involvement of the laity in the liturgical life of the Church, the reality proved something less than intended and in some ways was a bad thing. Language is the essential basis of the unity of a people and of societal stability. It is not only the cement that binds the building blocks but also a tribal and societal identifier. Without the unifying effect of language, cohesion in a society may be lost. Some African countries, for example, whose inhabitants speak well over a hundred different dialects, remain divided in many tribes rather than being an all-embracing, universal whole. Such divisions have led to armed, violent conflict and genocide. When a language is not understood it can be an alienating influence more potent than a unifying one. It can isolate a tribe in the ghetto and breed distrust, misunderstanding, discrimination, inter-tribal hatred, ignorance and violence, all damagingly disruptive to society.

Such division was not the case, however, in the pre-Vatican II Church even though the Latin was remote from all spoken languages in the world and not understood except by scholars of the language and Italian speakers to whom the Latin was familiar in the genesis of their spoken language. Practising Catholics around the world, regardless of where they lived or what language they spoke, all knew and understood the Latin of the Mass. From a very young age the pre-Vatican II Catholic read a missal in which the pages were divided down the middle with the Latin on one side and the corresponding vernacular on the other. It was never the case that the people of the Church didn't know what was going on because of a language barrier and that, therefore, the Latin language must be removed in favour of the local vernacular. Nevertheless, the changes in the format and language of the Mass did make it easier for the laity, and particularly children, to participate more fully. Such participation was, however, never sacerdotal nor was it intended to be.

Before Vatican II a Catholic could attend Mass anywhere in the world, a foreigner amongst a strange tribe, and feel completely at home without any knowledge or understanding of the local spoken language. Latin was the keystone of Catholicism supporting and locking the whole together as one. Although the teachings and dogma of Catholicism were universal, applying to all peoples regardless of their spoken language, the Latin of the Mass was the singular feature of universality that brought a visitor into communion with a society in which he was an alien. All peoples, regardless of race, tribe, language or the country in which they attended Mass to celebrate the Sacrament of Eucharist, the pinnacle of Christian practice and belief, were as one through the Latin. With the introduction of the vernacular, however, the universality which allowed belonging and unity amongst strangers has been lost. The abandonment of a unifying language has divided Catholicism into tribes defined not by their spiritual commonality in the Mass but by their diversity of culture, race, geography and language, that is, by their human characteristics. While this doesn't alter the essential essence of Catholicism, for the common man it is a great tragedy and was unnecessary.

Modern day Catholics who consider the Latin archaic and irrelevant and find the vernacular thus more apt to the modern day do not realise, never having attended a Latin Mass, that all pre-Vatican II Catholics understood the Latin Mass completely, perhaps even more completely, because they had to pay attention to the reading of the vernacular in order to keep up with the Latin of the liturgy. The necessity to read the vernacular printed in the missal alongside the Latin meant that the pre-Vatican II Catholic knew every prayer in the Mass backwards, including those that the priest prayed in silence. These silent prayers are still part of the Mass but never heard or read by the modern day Catholics and thus unknown to them. Indeed, although not actively involved in the ceremony attending the liturgy, pre-Vatican II Catholics were engrossed in the entire liturgy. Further, the sacred music exclusively prayed the Mass. Now, the intrusion of often childish hymn singing during the Mass drowns out much of the prayer of the Mass and many Catholics no longer hear nor know the prayers of the Mass, particularly those preliminary to the consecration, and sit there bored and not taking the interest and participation that Vatican II had intended.

Indeed, it is not unreasonable to suggest that the post-Vatican II Catholic laity rather than being included in the liturgy are now largely excluded with little participation in the ritual practice. This has been contributed to in no small measure by the failure of the Church for some four decades since the Council concluded to produce a new missal containing all the prayers of the Mass. Few modern day Catholics have any idea of what is being prayed in the Mass despite the great vernacular experiment. Even more damaging, however, is the intrusion of meaningless hymn singing rather than reverential silence in that part of the Mass immediately following reception of Holy Communion when a private communion with God in personal prayer should again be the preferred liturgical imperative as it was before the reforms of Vatican II. Indeed, it could be argued that modern day lay people are excluded from a large part of the liturgy rather than included as intended by Vatican II, are thoroughly bored because of that and, in consequence, can find much better things to do with their time than sitting in the pews on Sunday.

The change to the vernacular also meant that the sacred music shifted from the multisyllabic Latin language and the instrumentation which accompanied it with its cadences, mystique and grandeur to be replaced often by a more confined vocalisation and culturally more typical and available instrumentation. Vatican II, in the document *Sacrosanctum Concilium,* prescribed the nature of sacred music. The need for so-called enculturation of sacred music was recognised, e.g., use of the bongo drum or guitar in countries where such instrumentation elevated the peoples spirits rather than the traditional grand organ of most advanced English-speaking nations in the Western world. Music and song are potent stimulants of the human spirit and a great unifier.

Combined, these two inspire young men in war, move people to tears, stir memory, bring sadness or joy, manipulate emotions and attitudes, produce peace, reverence, foreboding, recklessness, abandonment and celebration. In contrast to the spoken vernacular, music and song are capable of elevating the human spirit towards God regardless of whether any accompanying language is understood or not.

The instrumental and sung liturgies have been greatly damaged in the modern Catholic Church in Australia and struggle or fail to achieve the uplifting effects of the sacred music of the pre-Vatican II era. Together with a loss of the perception of the special nature and mysticism of priesthood compared with the lay state, the emasculation of sacred music has contributed to the loss of that special spiritual dimension demanding reverence in the physical church – the house of God. Being in church no longer inspires silence, reverence, quiet prayer or meditation in many Catholic parish churches that have come to resemble social meeting halls similar to a shopping centre on Saturday morning. Many nominal Catholics in this day and age prefer the ambience of the village coffee shop or local plant nursery to the Mass on Sunday mornings, a great tragedy in the wake of changes in the sacred liturgy.

Accompanying the failure of large numbers of nominal Catholics to attend Mass in their local parish every Sunday is the consequent loss of socialisation amongst Catholics and with that, the loss of identifiable community. The liturgy of the Ordinary of the Mass[19] has become far too ordinary to inspire in many Australian parishes. It has come to mean very little if anything to a large body of Catholics including, sadly, vast numbers of young people born and baptised as Catholics and supposedly educated in Catholic schools. This is the greatest sadness for both Christianity and Catholicism and forebodes badly for the future of the Church.

---

19 The Ordinary of the Mass (the order or sequence of the ritual) is essentially a descriptive term for the liturgy of the celebration of the Sacrament of *Eucharist*.

The place of artworks and architecture in enhancement of the liturgy has also been tragically forgotten and abandoned. In most Australian Catholic churches built or redecorated since Vatican II, Catholicism is not as easily identifiable as it was in the pre-conciliar Church. Liturgical art and architecture are intended to bring people to, or to remind them of, the presence of God in the physical environment of the church. Some newer church buildings do that but such is relatively uncommon. Existing church buildings were modified early after Vatican II through the removal of magnificent altars and sanctuaries together with baptismal fonts and altar rails in the quest to bring the laity into the Holy of Holies. Such architectural changes destroyed the Holy of Holies. The sense of a specialness of that part of the church which contained the earthly embodiment of God himself in the sanctuary tabernacle was lost. The sanctuary was no longer approached in silent reverence to kneel at the altar rail to receive one's Creator God in Holy Communion with Him.

Magnificent statuary artworks, all depicting some significant event in the origins and journey of Christianity, another of the signatures of Catholicism, were removed in favour of the bland face of despondent, God-fearing Protestantism. Awe and reverence disappeared in favour of modern efficiency and art, much of the art bearing no resemblance to recognisable Christianity. The perceivable presence of God was lost, something that young post-Vatican II Catholics have perhaps never experienced and which no doubt contributes in no small measure to the lack of reverence and holiness in today's Catholic Church, a great disaster and one of the worst outcomes of Vatican II. True sanctuary, the sense of awareness of the presence of God and the awe, reverence and enfolding embrace inspired by that sense, no longer exists in many Catholic churches and is foreign particularly to most young, post-Vatican II Catholics. The reasons for this can be firmly attributed to the shredding of the colourfully embossed and rich fabric of the liturgy and the failure of education programs for both adults and children in the post-conciliar Church.

7

A Great Catastrophe

... parents are the prime educators of their children ...
Gravissium Educationis, Vatican II, 1965

The Church: an educational dinosaur?
All Catholic children in the pre-Vatican II Church were taught the fundamentals of Catholicism through catechesis, teaching by question and answer. Most children knew the answers to a prepared series of questions backwards, sometimes aided and inspired by a rap over the knuckles with a wooden ruler by a well-meaning nun. The first question in our little book, *The Catechism,* was, "Who made you?". "God made me" came the chorused reply. The second question was, "Why did God make you?" And as one we knew that "God made me to know him, to love him, to serve him in this life and to live happily with him forever in heaven." This is all that need ever have been taught. Herein is the kernel of the nut that is cracking a little in these dubiously enlightened, yet controversial and confused days. The difficulty was getting to know God. Once God was known, then it would clearly be a lot easier to love and serve him.

Getting to know God, as exhorted by *The Catechism*, is not really very difficult. It is like getting to know someone like Picasso. To know Picasso, a unique and singular artist, it is first necessary to study his works, not read an art appreciation book or his biography, although that might help. And then, even when the study is done, that does not necessarily bestow understanding of Picasso the artist-creator. So it is with the God-Creator. To know him is to know his works, not read some ancient Semite health ordinance or metaphorical explanation of creation or accounts of retributive theist vengeance in the Old Testament, but accounts of the life of Christ in the New Testament might help.

We on this Earth live each day surrounded by God's works and in our haste in pursuit of all that is temporal and fleeting don't even notice the beauty that surrounds us. The magpies praising the break of day, the melody of the butcher birds, the grandeur of the mountains, the power of the sea, each little flower that opens, the perfume in the spring breeze, all creatures from the giant blue whale to the microscopic, unicellular amoeba, each selfless person who holds out a helping hand to a brother or sister, who nurses the sick or uses personal talents to achieve great things for fellow human beings. It is in these works that God is to be found and in them there is much to love, much to serve, much to bring happiness to life on this Earth and reward not necessarily confined in the hereafter. When we know God's works, we might get to know God, but will also find much that we don't understand just as with Picasso. Simple observation of the world around us by any rational being devoid of mind-numbing self-absorption screams out, "Unbelief is impossible".

Unbelief plagues the post-Vatican II Catholic Church. In the 50 years since the Council, the world has seen the loss of an entire parental generation of un-informed Catholics evidenced by the lack of adherence to Catholic teaching and practice, largely perhaps because the current generation would seem to have little or no understanding of what those teachings and practice are, or alternatively, simply doesn't care. The children of that generation are even further removed from Catholicism despite many of them having been educated in nominal Catholic schools. The abandonment of the teaching of the tenets of the Catholic Faith after Vatican II may be related in no small way to the 30 year gap in the production of the new *Catechism of the Catholic Church,* including a version for children, and the failure to produce a new daily missal until recently. This gap was not adequately filled by adult education from the pulpits. Worse, however, was that preparatory teaching in Catholic schools was abandoned by those who traditionally took on this ministry in favour of embracing social justice in various guises, justifying their abandonment by reliance on the statement in the Council document, *Gravissimum Educationis* (Declaration on Christian Education, Pope Paul VI, 28 October 1965), "parents are the prime educators of their children" – prime examples or role models for living a Christian life certainly, but hardly the prime educators in matters about which the parents themselves knew little or nothing. The loss within one generation has been catastrophic.

The average modern Australian Catholic no longer has time for, or interest in, self-education in matters of Church teaching. Further, there seems to have been a reluctance on the part of many bishops and priests to engage in public debate or discourse on matters of morality. It would seem that many are afraid of criticism and lack the intestinal fortitude to stand up for what they and the Church profess. The societal destruction of practices such as abortion, euthanasia, profligate sexuality, secular feminism and vexing areas of Catholic teaching such as contraception, same-sex marriage, ordination of women to the priesthood and life creating technologies such as cloning, surrogacy, embryonic stem cell research and in vitro fertilisation (IVF) are never embraced in the pulpits nor in regularly available education programs at the parish level.

For some reason which defies understanding, the Catholic people, that is the human Church, have been informed on these controversial issues by a largely uninformed and unsympathetic secular press, ignorant of Catholic moral teaching, rather than by the highly informed position of the Magisterium of their Church. Such is the abandonment of education in the modern Australian Church and, indeed, almost certainly contributes to an acceptance in the Catholic laity and in some religious and clergy of the "human compassion", "personal spirituality" and "human dignity" that have come to override morality in such matters. The educational silence of the post-Vatican II Church echoes a complete loss of faith in Christ and his teachings. In today's Church, knowledge of Catholic teaching is sadly lacking and until that is corrected the Church can only stumble on without repair or renovation towards a self-inflicted demise.

In the second sentence of its introduction, *Gravissimum Educationis* states: "Indeed, the circumstances of our time have made it easier and at once more urgent to educate young people and, what is more, to continue the education of adults." The Council clearly recognised the need to use the newly available modern aids that make education much easier and to apply these in its continuing education mission to adults and children. Compared with the other Vatican II documents, *Gavissimum Educationis* was in the main a reaffirmation of commitment to religious education and not an advocate for change. Nevertheless, after Vatican II educational changes came thick and fast and have contributed very little good, if any, to ongoing education of adults or children in the teachings and practice of Catholicism. Indeed, it is far easier to argue that changes after Vatican II have destroyed Catholic education.

The abandonment of the education of Catholic children and laity in the post-conciliar Church in Australia defies explanation and is indeed scandalous. This abandonment has exposed the people to the unopposed philosophical dictums of secular atheism, humanism, feminism, materialism and the cult of self that pervades modern society. They have been seduced by the popular, easily exonerating influences of caring for the "dignity" of human living and "social justice" both of which appear to take little account of personal responsibility. Many Catholics can no longer find a satisfying reason to follow Catholicism with its moral dictums that interfere with personal freedoms, particularly in matters of sexual practice. The concept of immoral behaviour (sin) is unpalatable in the modern world. The so-called dignity of human life in the secular society allows the right to abortion, euthanasia, same-sex marriage and anything else a particular individual desires.

The blame in this debacle, which can only be described as a betrayal of the Church, resides either with the Catholic education offices or with local delegated authority in the schools. Regardless of which is to blame, Vatican II affirmed the bishops, pastors of their flock, as the primary local authority, still subject, however, to papal authority. The bishops have to be answerable for this situation. *Gravissimum Educationis* states: "This sacred synod recalls to pastors of souls their most serious obligation to see to it that all the faithful but especially the youth who are the hope of the Church enjoy this Christian education" (10) and further, "But let teachers recognise that the Catholic school depends upon them almost entirely for the accomplishment of its goals and programs" (27). It is to be noted that the Council recognised that the education of school children depends on school teachers "almost entirely" and not on the parents as the "prime educators of their children" in the matters of formal Christian education.

Catholic schools are afraid to impose moral imperatives on their teachers, many of whom are not Catholic, who are supposed to teach the faith, if not in lessons, then at least through a Christian lifestyle example as with the obligation of parents as the prime educators. In Australia, this is in some part a consequence of the implementation of civil anti-discrimination law. The Church can be held to be in breach of the law if it insists on employing practising Catholic teachers in its schools or if it were to dismiss a staff member for serious behavioural breaches contrary to Catholic teaching and moral example to the school students. Such law is conveniently and paradoxically not considered discriminatory against the freedom of religious practice and education. Catholic schools in Australia today, regardless of the compulsory, erudite mission statements, are rarely identifiable other than through their names or past history and occasional lip service to

Catholicism in what are essentially social gatherings posing under the umbrella of various group and class Masses, enthusiastically attended by parents and students both, unlike Mass on the following Sunday. Catholic children at many schools no longer have a prayer life which is indeed the domain of both the school and the parents as prime educators.

There are of course those schools which do not fit this mould but they are few and far between and even the vast majority of their past students fail to regularly practise or defend their nominal Catholic faith, a daunting task when the majority know very little about that faith. The apologetics and theological study that were once a feature of Catholic secondary schools have disappeared and been replaced by compulsory religious studies as a points earning contribution to secular university entrance scores. Many Catholics emerge from this deception knowing more about other exotic, pagan and non-Catholic religions than about Catholicism. If it were not so destructive of the two richest and enduring traditions in the world to date, Catholicism and Judaism, it would be laughable. Indeed, Catholic education both for adults and children is laughable in Australia and represents perhaps the biggest post-Vatican II failing in the Catholic Church.

According to the account of Christ's life recorded by the apostolic, ordained priest, Matthew the Evangelist, Christ came to his priests (eleven of the original apostles) in the early days following his resurrection from death and commissioned them to go to all peoples in all nations teaching the people all that he had taught and revealed to them.[20] The failure of Catholic education in promulgating Christ's teachings and defending those teachings in the public domain since Vatican II is damningly contrary to and defies the clear primacy of

---

[20] Matt. 28:19-20: "Go then, to all peoples everywhere and make them my disciples, baptising them in the name of the Father, the Son and the Holy Spirit, and teach them to obey everything I have commanded you. And I will be with you always to the end of the age."

place and responsibility of the role of the clergy in education, as reaffirmed by Vatican II in *Gravissimum Educationis*. That role at the diocesan level is primarily the responsibility of the bishops.

It is true that the Australian Catholic Bishops Conference regularly expounds Catholic teaching in letters, documents and press releases, intended for education on Catholic teaching as it is applied to the world at large. Such releases are available in the Catholic churches, both in their original format and in the Catholic press, but are read by few, even of those Catholics who attend these churches, a number which today is a mere 10% or less of nominal Catholics. The remainder are informed if at all by the written press and electronic media, both addicted to sensational bites often critical of the Church and often proffered by self-appointed Catholic spokespersons employed in the media, hardly unbiased or necessarily educated opinions when their livelihoods depend on the sensationalism their efforts generate. This is the educational medium available to over 90% of today's nominal Catholics in Australia. These souls represent the biggest mission field for Catholicism in this country. The time is long overdue that the education of the disillusioned Catholic and Catholic children, rather than indulgence in feel-good distractions such as much of social justice practice, becomes the priority of the Church administration.

8

HUMAN SEXUALITY

The lust of the flesh directs sexual desires to satisfaction of the body, often at the cost of a real and full communion of persons

Pope John Paul II

Sexuality, marriage, priestly celibacy

Sexuality is an exciting, alluringly packaged gift from God the Creator. It does not, however, come with unfettered licence but with obligation and responsibility, simply, because it is the means through which God creates human life. It attests to God's trust in men and women as his instrument of human life creation and the remarkable privilege that entails. This great gift comes without an owner's manual but with built-in accessories, such as the instincts for right and wrong and for the nurturing and protection of human life. This instinctive human awareness or in-built moral code embodies what is known as the natural law and goes hand in hand with a discretionary will which can control its usage.

Of necessity, sexuality produces perhaps the most potent of all human desires and needs. This is indeed an essential of sexuality since if desires for consummation were not potent or were easily overridden by will, procreation might well not be sufficient to maintain human life in this world. But therein lies a great paradox. The potency of the desires of human sexuality, designed to stimulate the need for procreation, often overrides stewardship of this great gift and in the human being too frequently becomes the progenitor of conflict and human distress, when God's intent is the very opposite. The pleasure that attends human sexual consummation is so seductive that the act of sexual intercourse in the human as opposed to all other animals becomes the servant of pleasure rather than the servant of procreation of life.

Sexuality cannot logically exist independently of procreation when it is the very orchestrator and essence of that privileged function, the only reason for the existence of the sexes, of man and woman. Such positioning of the place of sexuality in human life by the Catholic Church and its insistence that sexuality be used for its intended purpose clearly places restriction on the unfettered human response to carnal desire. Catholic teaching does not condemn carnal desire. What the Catholic Church does teach is that this God-given gift, in the fact of its role in creating human life, is yet another outward sign of God amongst men, that is, sacramental, and has formalised this act of creation within the Sacrament of Matrimony. In practical terms, this fundamental Catholic concept of the sanctity of procreative human life can exist only within a marriage between a man and a woman which accepts the responsibility of stewardship of any human life which arises from their procreative coupling. In this basic teaching exists so much of the criticism, derision and controversy that plagues Catholicism, the biggest and most enduring single testament to Christianity in the modern world and the creator of marriage as it is understood in Western civilisation.

Such criticism is understandable and to be expected of those pagan and atheistic elements ignorant of Catholic teaching. Paradoxically, however, much of it is forthcoming from professed Catholics including clergy and much of Protestantism and its clergy in the name of Christianity. Professed Catholics and would-be Catholic reformers and renewalists who seek to secularise Catholic Christianity do so because of the omissions of the Catholic education system, replaced in the modern world by the opinions of a secular press unfamiliar with Catholicism's tenets Clergy and the fleet of commentators, Catholic and otherwise, critical of the Church's position on sexuality can only be explained by their desire to be accepted by a secular world or alternatively by a loss of faith. Culpable again is the Church itself which has failed to counter those secular commentators in the public domain who influence the uneducated by the proffering of unfounded opinion as truth.

In Catholic teaching, marriage is a God-sanctified event mediated through the Sacrament of Matrimony, where a man and a woman formalise a partnership or union with God the Creator as instruments of the creation of human life. The marriage covenant (contract)[21] carries with it the moral obligation to care for any human life, both temporally and spiritually, that may arise from the sexual union, but does not demand that procreation must follow marriage. Rather, the marriage covenant demands that the opportunity for creation of life must be permitted, that is, that the partners in marriage are morally obliged to consummate their union through sexual intercourse between the man and woman as ordered through the natural law. Marriage also carries civic responsibility to human dignity and the ordering of society to the common good. Thus, same-sex marriage does not fit in with Catholic teaching which recognises that homosexual relationships do not form part of that mechanism through which human life comes into being. Thus the Catholic disconnect with same-sex marriage is based on the exclusion of the purpose and intent of sexual union as an instrument of God's creation of human life. It follows then that Catholic moral teaching does not and cannot within the realms of rational argument support homosexual unions whether of men or women under the guise of marriage.

In simple terms, de facto means evident in the fact but not the real thing. It is a term that might well be used to describe a very good, fake diamond. The term "de facto marriage" is applied to a

---

21 A covenant differs from a contract in that it is immutable and endures forever, whereas a contract can be modified, manipulated, legally challenged or terminated.

heterosexual couple living together in fact, not in marriage but in a simulation thereof, and may reasonably be applied to any couple living together in a consensual sexual relationship, both heterosexual and homosexual. Heterosexual de facto relationships are recognised in the civil law in many Western countries and essentially attract the same civil rights as do marriage relationships. Marriage has always been recognised in civil law in our society – an example of the role of the law in the ordering of a civilised society. While the Catholic Church recognises that many de facto partners take an exemplary place in society as faithful partners and parents of children to whom they extend great care and love, that does not equate with altering its fundamental understanding of God the Creator's intent of sexual practice. In defining the fundamentals of moral law as applied to sexual relationships, although many modern day Catholics clamour for change in the Church's teachings, there is no room for the accommodation of reform, renewal or change which denies the basic morality of those teachings. That does not mean that the Catholic Church shuns or refuses to accept homosexual individuals or those in de facto relationships, homosexual or heterosexual, in the Church. It simply means that the Church through study of scripture, tradition and an understanding of the natural law has prescribed the moral position to which the followers of Christ should subscribe.

Homosexual couples today seek recognition of their sexuality based relationship as a formalised marriage. Such an ambition is clearly to establish homosexuality as an accepted norm of our society and a legitimate vehicle for parenting a family. Parentage in a genetic sense is clearly not a logical accompaniment of homosexual union. In the same way that homosexual marriage is best classified as de facto marriage for purposes of recognition of certain rights and privileges in civil law, the custodial parenting or nurturing of children as opposed to genetic parentage by homosexual couples is also de facto. This does not demean the caring of children by a homosexual couple any more than it does the same caring by a de facto heterosexual couple, since both demand the same commitment and self-sacrifice as does parenting within heterosexual formalised marriage.

However, the biological fact is that a parent contributes to the very genetic being of a child and homosexual couples regardless of any contrived rhetoric cannot claim parentage as a result of homosexual union. They can, however, claim foster parentage as do heterosexual couples who are unable to conceive a child but who offer responsible and loving care to an otherwise parentless child. For a homosexual couple to claim anything other or to demand anything other is clearly ridiculous and disordered thinking and demands sympathy rather than criticism. A woman in a homosexual relationship can conceive a child, clearly not from her partner, but through an unknown or chosen male sperm donor and use of IVF technology or through heterosexual intercourse with a chosen male employed specifically for the purpose. Clearly the non-contributing partner has no claim to genuine parentage but in the experience of nurturing care can claim de facto parentage. For both to claim parentage, however, is supremely sad and such pretence cannot possibly be viewed as an alternative normalcy within human society and is bound to cause future confusion for a child parented in such an arrangement when the child grows to an age where an understanding of the world at large becomes apparent.

The quest for the acceptance of homosexual practice as a normalcy of human behaviour by the homosexual community is, in its very existence, evidence of that innate instinctive recognition of the natural law, characteristic of the human being in contrast to all other life – an unavoidable recognition of the abnormal nature of homosexual practice. In simple terms, the plea for acceptance of the normalcy of homosexuality betrays the fact that the homosexual community itself recognises instinctively the abnormalcy of homosexual practice. Otherwise, the campaign for normalcy would not exist. The plea for normalcy should not be met with the moralising self-righteousness and evangelisation of fundamentalist Christianity nor should it be accommodated by civil legislation which seeks to establish a basic wrong as a human right or an aberrancy as a normality.

Elevation of homosexuality to a mainstream level of acceptance that transcends any consideration of wrong-doing or violation of human life is not a new phenomenon. It was the common practice of prominent men in ancient Greek and Roman societies to 'marry' young boys for sexual gratification even when living in a concurrent heterosexual relationship. These societies were steeped in profligate sexual activity characterised amongst other behaviours by public orgies and also an erosion of ethical standards accompanied by violence and lack of respect for human life, manifested by self-mutilation practices, increasing suicide rates, homosexuality and violent destruction of human life performed as entertainment in such sanguine theatres as the murderous Coliseum in Rome. Today's society has seen a meteoric rise in self-mutilation, youth suicide, homosexuality and sanguine entertainments in the electronic Coliseums, television and the movie theatre. These behaviours accompanied the steady decline and final demise of the Greek and Roman empires. This is an apt description of Western society today, particularly in the most powerful and affluent nations, led in the main by the United States of America and the United Kingdom, and followed by their compliant lapdogs in countries like Australia. Today it is not unreasonable to speculate that we in our society are living through a similar decline.

Homosexuality is a matter of great controversy and confusion. Acceptance of homosexuality vocalised as Christian charity and understanding does not accord with Catholic teaching, but in saying that, neither does Catholic teaching exclude charity and understanding towards homosexual individuals. Indeed, in those times when moralistic biblical perceptions of homosexuality dictated oppressive, punitive civil law and Christian societal persecution, even to the point of violent physical abuse, such actions did not accord with Catholic teaching concerning the sanctity of all human life. Further it did not accord with the teaching that urges forgiveness, not condemnation of others whom God loves as he does all humanity despite its failings or flaws. However, it would be disingenuous to suggest that there are not professed Catholics who possess un-Christian attitudes towards homosexual people in keeping with the mores of a society which has a historical background of persecution of homosexuals within the framework of a somewhat hypocritical English punitive morality and civil law, even though that law has been abolished in more enlightened times.

Thus, Catholic teaching on homosexuality is not based on the regulatory legal, health, lifestyle and behavioural musings of the biblical Old Testament writer Leviticus,[22] nor on the account of God's retributive destruction of Sodom because of its male homosexual activities which contributed the word sodomy to the lexicon.[23] These Old Testament stories pre-date Christianity but nevertheless remain in the armamentarium of fundamentalist Protestant clerical attack on homosexual people. Catholic teaching on homosexual practice, whether between men or women, is based on the fundamental premise of the creative nature of sexual intercourse and in moral terms can be categorised in precisely the same way as heterosexual intercourse outside marriage, whether that be consensual or not. In other words, the immorality that Catholic teaching applies to homosexual intercourse is no different from that which applies to heterosexual intercourse outside marriage. The immorality exists in the fundamental misuse of the life-creating intent of sexual intercourse.

---

22 No man is to have sexual relations with another man; God hates that (Leviticus 18:22).
23 Suddenly the Lord rained burning sulphur on the cities of Sodom and Gomorrah and destroyed them and the whole valley, along with all the people there and everything that grew on the land (Genesis 19:24-25).

Catholic morality demands that any sexual activity which precludes the intended outcome of sexual intercourse, that is, the creation of human life, is immoral in its practice.

In the questionably advanced Western world in countries such as the United States and Australia, Catholic homosexuals and bisexuals have banded together in an international organisation known as the Rainbow Sash Movement, whose members militantly proclaim their sexual freedom to indulge in their preference for sexual gratification which they view as a variation of normalcy of human life. Thus, within the Catholic Church they claim a right to receive the Sacraments of the Church, most notably, Eucharist (Holy Communion). In Australia, the actions of Cardinal George Pell towards members of the Australian arm of the international Rainbow Sash Movement, were a matter of some controversy and confusion involving great personal vilification, derision and disrespect towards the then Archbishop of Sydney and the Church, sadly from many Catholics.

In early 2002, an organised demonstration by members of the movement invaded a Mass being celebrated by Dr George Pell in St Patrick's Cathedral when he was Archbishop of Melbourne. It is Catholic teaching that in the Sacrament of the Eucharist, the very core of Catholicism and Christianity, God the Creator consecrates (sanctifies) bread and wine through the ministry of his priest and in so doing alters the essence of these without observable change in physical form to contain God's presence therein (the "Real Presence"). Those who partake of both or either of the bread and wine in the Sacrament of Eucharist are in communion with God himself. Should a person deliberately receive the consecrated bread and wine in a state of alienation from his Creator God through abandonment of morality, in a spirit which denies reverence due to God, or for a purpose other than sacred union with Christ (for example, to make a political or social statement), then, such an act is sacrilegious and in itself immoral. A Catholic priest is morally obliged to deny reception of the consecrated bread and wine to any such person if he has genuine reason to believe that an intending recipient is alienated from God and not in a "state of grace".

The Rainbow Sash Movement in Melbourne marched in procession into St Patrick's Cathedral draped in their rainbow sashes, a frank admission of their active homosexual practice, and demanded that Archbishop Pell distribute Holy Communion to them. This was a political statement and an affirmation that they disapproved of the Church teachings on human sexuality, in particular homosexuality. The Archbishop in his judgement of the events determined that the act was sacrilegious (violation or profanation of something sacred) and refused to distribute the Eucharist to the protesters. Had the Archbishop succumbed to their demands he would have been in breach of his own moral obligation as an ordained priest. This episode caused a great public outcry and criticism of Archbishop Pell. What he did was an act of great bravery for which he was vilified and disrespected ever since. His subsequent appointment and arrival in Sydney as Archbishop was accompanied by a media blitz by the homosexual community of Sydney through letters in the printed press and echoed throughout other media outlets, typically by commentators ignorant of Catholic teaching.

Members of the Rainbow Sash Movement in Sydney have also presented themselves before the Archbishop to receive Holy Communion which he refused. In his actions, however, Archbishop Pell did not exclude homosexuals from the Church as he consistently blessed these activists (that is, extended God's acceptance within the human and Christian family) who appeared before him demanding reception of Holy Communion. Homosexuals and heterosexuals alike who flaunt and refuse God's teachings as prescribed by Christianity, are by implication not in full communion with the Church but are indeed self-alienated through their actions. In their alienation they are not excluded or exiled from the Church but full communion with the Church, embodied in the Eucharist, is dependent on acceptance of the moral obligations required. Catholics are excluded from the reception of the Eucharist if they are known to have committed other breaches of moral law such as murder, rape, adultery and larceny. Thus, having a tendency towards homosexual activity, in the same way that having a tendency towards rape or any other immorality, does not in itself exclude a person from the Church. Such persons remain in full communion until they engage in active immoral practices. Should that happen, the person is not in full communion until such time as they are restored through God's forgiveness in the Sacrament of Reconciliation. Such forgiveness is dependent, however, on the resolution and commitment not to repeat their breaches of moral law. This is the kernel of Catholic teaching on homosexuality. Those who do not accept it are not to be judged by men. Such judgement within Catholicism is God's domain and his alone.

One of the major marriage-related controversies hounding modern Catholicism is priestly celibacy, the state of being unmarried, not as many wrongly understand it as a state of sexual chastity or abstinence. No normal celibate person, priest or otherwise, is devoid of human sexual desire. Celibacy in the Catholic priesthood has applied during most of the last millennium. The Catholic priest is held to the same moral tenets as all others of Catholic adherence, namely, that the human procreative act of sexual intercourse should be confined within the framework of sacramental marriage. Clearly, in the moral teaching of the Catholic Church, the celibate state precludes sexual intercourse in the ordained priesthood, yet another covenant of man with God through the Sacrament of Holy Orders.

The life of the priest is ideally based on the life of Christ, a male celibate priest. Christ, before his death, commissioned (ordained) his twelve apostles, all males, to act as priests in his name and in memory of him. There is nothing in the Gospel accounts of Jesus' life that indicates that he was in any way anti-women, possessed of an overwhelmingly male chauvinism or misogyny. Indeed, the Gospels indicate that Jesus was a champion and liberator of women. He forgave the woman "taken in adultery" and prevented her being stoned to death. He freed the divorced woman at the well of the vilification that dogged her; women were numbered amongst his closest friends; he stopped in his agonising journey towards his death by crucifixion to speak to the women of Jerusalem and healed women in compassion and loved them as he did all human beings. He knew many women according to the Gospels and many of them were his faithful and loyal followers. However, he did not ordain any of them to his priesthood. I can't presume to suggest the reason, but can understand why celibacy became part of the Catholic priesthood and was adopted by many others, both male and female, who chose a life of service to God as unordained members of the many religious communities within the Catholic Church.

That the Second Vatican Council did not change the Church's position on priests marrying might well have contributed in some part to the exodus of large numbers of Catholic priests living through the liberated times of the 1960s and 1970s. Generations of young Catholic men since then, largely uneducated in the teachings of their Church and seduced by the freedoms of the new world, particularly the sexual freedoms, could find little inspiration to aspire to the priesthood. This, combined with the attrition that inevitably accompanies the passage of time, has produced a dearth of ministering Catholic priests in the developed countries and the gaps that grow year by year in Australia are inadequately filled by priests mainly from foreign cultures in the largely undeveloped world who often possess little understanding of the ethos of the people or of modern Western society, even though many are very good priests and pastors of their people.

In the last decade increasing numbers of married Protestant clergymen, some with families, have embraced Catholicism in a philosophical shift not dissimilar to that of the Oxford Movement.

In consequence, the Catholic Church has embraced their desires for reconciliation and reunion with Catholicism and has admitted the ordination of some ministers in the Catholic priesthood. There now exist both married and celibate priests. It may well be that this is a prelude to change in the policy of priestly celibacy in the future for unmarried young men who might wish to become priests and, if so, will become a major factor in the numerical restoration of ministry which is an urgent need for the modern Catholic Church. Administrative policies that govern the Catholic Church, unlike its moral tenets, are not immutable. Celibacy is not a moral tenet of priesthood. The moral tenet which attaches to priesthood is that a priest should not indulge in sexual intercourse outside God's intended purpose, the creation of human life in union with God within the Sacrament of Marriage. There is, however, little doubt that the Catholic Church will lose some mysticism and authority in the eyes of its people should celibacy be removed from the priesthood. The priest will not enjoy the same place in society as he currently does. He will become too like ordinary men rather than like Christ.

Celibacy has in recent times become increasingly controversial in the light of the revelations of sexual abuse by priests of adults and particularly children, both male and female. In the opinions of many critics and commentators, celibacy has been suggested as a major contributing cause. It is interesting that the magnitude of this diabolical scourge, like the sexual revolution itself, post-dates Vatican II. According to the Irish inquiry into sexual abuse by clergy concluded after a decade of hearings, this scourge demonstrated in the Dublin Archdiocese an increase in incidence from 2% to 9% across the 1940s and 1950s and from the mid-'60s a progressive increasing incidence, decade by decade, to a peak of 38% by the end of the 1980s. This peak incidence was followed by a precipitous fall to 9% in the 1990s and to 2% over the first decade of this century, in a time when people are more inclined to report abuse but also when perhaps numbers involved with an active Church life have fallen. (The percentages quoted refer not to the number of priests in the Dublin Archdiocese but to the number of reported cases of sexual abuse).[24] It may not be too disingenuous to suggest that this extraordinary acceleration in sexual abuse by Catholic clergy was perpetrated by priests who chose not to join the post-Vatican II exodus and were denied the sexual liberation they had either expected or hoped for in allowing clergy to marry. Others might suggest that it was the result of increased reporting by victims, and others, that perhaps some victims were fabricating their experiences, both highly unlikely propositions. Of greater credence is the fact that the Catholic hierarchy closeted the problem through fear of increasing loss of respect for its clergy and the Church. Whatever the cause, however, there is no evidence which establishes celibacy in the priesthood as the primary cause of child sexual abuse. Indeed, the enquiries into child sexual abuse have shown that this heinous practice is widespread throughout all institutions and thus far more likely to be perpetrated in all other religious and secular institutions by people not confined by celibacy, an exclusive requirement of Catholic priesthood. Further, enquiries have shown that child sexual abuse is far more common within families (up to 90% of all child abuse in some surveys) and more likely to be perpetrated by the non-celibate.

Justice Murphy in her report of abuse in the Irish Catholic Church expressed a view that the administration in the post-Vatican II Church failed to apply its own canon law. It seems that if that is the case, the administrative mechanisms of the Church chose to hide the truth in the interests of preventing damage that revelation might inflict, rather than applying the law of God embodied in its own moral teaching.

---

24 Vatican representatives appearing before a hearing of the United Nations Committee on the Rights of Children in Geneva, on 16 January 2014, said that the Vatican continues to receive around 600 complaints against abusive priests every year, many dating back to the 1960s, 1970s and 1980s, the post-Vatican II period corresponding with the great acceleration in abuse revealed by the findings in the Irish inquiry.

In other words the administrative machinery overrode God's moral law. This was possibly a greater disillusionment with the Church than the sexual abuse itself and caused an accelerating exodus of large numbers of Catholics. The presence of God amongst men, the very essence of sacramental Catholicism ministered through the ordained priesthood, is the basis of the respect in which the Catholic priesthood is held within Catholicism. Just as any human being in a state of moral alienation from God's law is excluded from the sacraments even more so should a proven abusing priest be excluded from the ministry of those sacraments and not permitted to continue his ministry in another diocese as has happened in the administrative management of this problem.

The corruption of the priesthood by sexually abusing clergy is the greatest weapon that could ever be used to destroy the Catholic Church and has gone very close to achieving just that. The great imperative in the matter of sexual abuse for the Church is to expel, or defrock, the priest perpetrators, denying them a role in the sacramental ministry, according to its own canon law.[25] Further, the imperative is that these reported child abusers should be tried under civil law and either exonerated or sentenced under that law. It is not the philosophy or teaching of the Catholic Church that is the problem in the matter of sexual abuse by clergy but rather the failure of the immoral abusing priest himself and of the man-made administrative authorities of the Church in response to that immoral behaviour. The abrogation of moral administrative responsibility has orchestrated the great clamour for administrative change.

---

25 In a further hearing of the United Nations Committee in Geneva in May 2014, Vatican representatives said that 848 priests had been defrocked and 2572 others punished, representing the total number of cases brought to attention over the last decade, many of those dating back to earlier decades, predominantly the 1960s, 70s and 80s.

9

Contraception

*Conception is the implantation
of a fertilised ovum in the womb*

**American College of Obstetricians
and Gynecologists, 1972**

A damaging misconception

Contraception is perhaps the one issue where Catholic teaching is not accepted by many Catholics living in a world where everyone else considers it an accepted, necessary norm of responsible heterosexual behaviour and management of a dependent family within the limits imposed by both personal and financial responsibility. Since Pope Paul VI's encyclical *Humanae Vitae* of 1968, which reaffirmed the teaching on contraception, there has been ever decreasing adherence to it by the Catholic community. Many surveys have suggested that up to 80% of nominal Catholics disagree with the teaching that the exclusion of God's creative purpose, that is, the procreation of human life in sexual intercourse, through the use of artificial means intended to frustrate that procreation, is immoral. Such a practice is contrary to the natural law and is peculiar to the human being as opposed to all other procreative life in this world.

Artificial means include the contraceptive pill and the morning after pill, condoms, diaphragms, intrauterine contra-implantation devices, surgical sterilisation of either man or woman and a menagerie of imaginative alternatives which are intended to make conception and implantation of a fertilised ovum in the womb impossible. It should be noted that the intention to frustrate the procreation of human life means precisely that and does not mean, for instance, the intention to prevent sexually transmitted disease, a matter of considerable criticism of the Church in relation to condoms as a protection against AIDS and other sexually transmitted diseases. It was met by a typical outcry of journalistic ignorance around the world when Pope John Paul II intimated that there was not necessarily an objection within Catholic teaching to the use of condoms when the intention was not to prevent life but rather serious life-threatening disease. The exclusion of God's creative purpose, contrary to the natural law and thus inherently immoral, is the fundamental basis of the Church's moral teachings on this vexed, controversial, confused and poorly understood issue, both inside and outside the Church. The Church cannot change the natural law and its position on contraception is thus immutable. However, there is a need to seriously review the degrees of immorality that apply to contraception by acceptance of the revelations of science in the modern age, something unavailable at the time when the teachings on contraception were originally promulgated. The revelations of science are truth and thus are revelations of God's creation. The Church has an obligation, therefore, to re-address these revelations and establish their application to living a moral life in the modern world.

Far from retreating into a defensive fortress, the Catholic Church was in fact the first and only opponent of the sexual revolutionary forces to investigate, to become informed and to examine the appropriateness of its own moral position on the matter of contraception. Under the guidance of Pope Paul VI, the Church undertook a wide-ranging enquiry into contraception. A medical advisory committee of over 70 experts, (many of whom were not Catholics), including scientists, doctors, obstetricians, gynaecologists, the American inventor of 'the pill' and lay persons deliberated over the matter and advised the Vatican. In response, Pope Paul wrote the encyclical *Humanae Vitae* ("Of Human Life"). This encyclical (a statement of Catholic moral teaching), subtitled *On the Regulation of Birth*, was promulgated on the

25 July 1968 and reaffirmed the traditional teaching regarding human sexual love within marriage, responsible parenthood and the rejection of artificial means of contraception. Groans of disappointment echoed throughout Catholicism at a time when the pop culture of free love, drug-induced ecstasy and the birth of radical feminism with its bra burning and trashing of all that revered and respected women, proclaimed the new found sexual freedom and derided the Catholic teaching against artificial contraception which denied women safe participation in the sexual freedom that contraception permitted.

For some reason, which again defies understanding, the Catholic people, that is the human Church, were informed on contraception by a largely uninformed and unsympathetic secular press, ignorant of Catholic moral teaching, rather than by the highly informed position of the Vatican expressed by Pope Paul VI. The reporting in the secular press ignored those qualifications in Catholic teaching which modified the dogmatic statement of the unqualified ban on all artificial contraception regardless of other moral considerations in producing a child, and which were thus not newsworthy, not sensational and provided no basis for attack on the Catholic Church. The reporting of *Humanae Vitae* ignored completely all other modifiers applicable to all Catholic teaching across the panorama of multiple situation differences and variations in the living of human life and the ordering of human society. For example, there was never any mention in the secular press of the following direct quote from Pope Paul's *Humanae Vitae* encyclical: "With regard to physical, economic, psychological and social conditions, responsible parenthood is exercised by those who prudently and generously decide for serious reasons and with due respect to moral precepts, not to have additional children for either a certain or an indefinite period of time."

It is Catholic teaching that a genuinely informed conscience may have primacy over dogmatic teaching in some circumstances. An informed conscience is one that knows and considers moral law and teaching in making a moral decision for a particular action based on the greater morality of an outcome balanced against the morality of the means to achieve that outcome. Such a moral decision that may seem to be contrary to the letter of dogma does not transgress Catholic moral law and teaching. In other words, moral practice genuinely arrived at in favour of a greater good does admit some variability in keeping with the vast variability of human circumstance. Such variability might be expressed as a variability in the degree or depth of moral transgression inherent in the practice of contraception in certain circumstances. Catholic people in the main seemed unaware of these teachings and the Church made no effort to promote an understanding of them. The changing times, however, seemed to the Catholic laity to be leaving them behind, dinosaurs in a rapidly improving world. And so the clamour for change echoed around the Catholic world.

In the aftermath of the release of *Humanae Vitae*, the British media, both print and television, were awash with discussion and opinion pieces on Catholic opposition to contraception. At the same time, the sectarian Catholic/Protestant bloody and lethal battles on the city streets of British Northern Ireland between the provisional Irish Republican Army (IRA) and the British Army were graphically brought into every living room in the United Kingdom by the BBC. Some of the most damning television images coming out of this contrived sectarian war were those of young children hurling stones, Molotov cocktails and profanities at the British forces patrolling the streets, inflicting injury and death. In a BBC television panel discussion on Pope Paul's encyclical, *Humanae Vitae*, the English Catholic Cardinal, John Heenan, expressed the opinion that the media perceptions of Church teaching were largely uninformed and did not, as widely suggested, represent an uncaring imposition of archaic Church law on a suffering Catholic laity. Cardinal Heenan offered an explanation of his opinion by outlining the moral responsibility demanded of Catholic parents as the obligation to take stewardship of both the temporal and moral wellbeing of any child for whom they were responsible through procreative sexual union. He illustrated this teaching with the example of a Belfast Catholic mother with a large family and a violent, drunken husband who imposed his sexual will on her according to his whim.

The Cardinal said that if the woman believed in all conscience that in the environment in which she and her children lived she could not care for her children's moral wellbeing and was not prepared to bring another child into that environment, then the moral responsibility towards the children permitted the practice of contraception, if necessary by taking the pill, particularly if the practice of natural means of preventing conception based on co-operation by both parties was impossible in a violent marriage in which the mother was unable to prevent unwanted sexual intercourse. This signal event led to widespread contraceptive practice using the pill within Catholicism in England in the assurance that a properly informed, non-contrived conscience could determine individual, morally acceptable practice based on the principle of justifiable means towards a better moral end, a concept which applies across the spectrum of Catholic teaching and contributes, for example, to the justification of war in the protection of human life even though some life will be lost in the process.

The Church's teaching on contraception is by no means new. Indeed, the Old Testament condemns contraception as contrary to God's law and all Christianity had done so until the Anglican Conference of Lambeth in 1930 when the Anglican Church formally permitted artificial contraception. Some Western Christian societies had banned contraception under civil law until as recently as the mid-20th century. Other Protestant denominations soon followed the Anglican position after the Lambeth Conference, leaving the Catholic

Church as the sole adherent to the concept of the fundamental immorality of frustrating God's creative purpose and intention through all contraceptive measures considered to be contrary to the natural law. A reform of the teaching on contraception is a major demand from many of the modern day reformers and renewalists. Since the processes surrounding contraception were not fully understood scientifically until the mid 20th century, perhaps the time has come for the teaching on contraception to be revisited and either affirmed yet again or modified.

"When does life begin?" dictates the moral and ethical debate on such matters as contraception and abortion. The answer has always been, "At conception". It was not until the 20th century, however, when medical science advanced through microscopy and a knowledge of hormones and their effects on human tissues that the processes involved in conception were accurately identified. It is now known that pregnancy results from: first, fertilisation of an ovum to form a multifunctional human cell known as a zygote; second, the zygote's development to the blastocyst stage; third, the successful implantation of the blastocyst in a receptive lining of a woman's womb. Each of these three stages, although wonderfully co-ordinated in one seamless process, is in fact separate in its individual implication for the inevitable formation of human life.

The fertilised ovum faces a perilous journey of some 6-7 days, which it may or may not survive, during which it repeatedly divides to form the multicellular blastocyst before it is implanted in the womb to become the embryo. Human life is not inevitable with fertilisation of an ovum, neither is it inevitable with development to the blastocyst stage, both of which processes take place outside the womb in the abdominal cavity and in the Fallopian tube. Thus, although the fertilised ovum is living and identifiably human in its cellular characteristics, for at least 6-7 days from the time of fertilisation it does not represent the established *inevitability* of human life but rather, like the unfertilised ovum and spermatozoon themselves, the *potential* for human life which might never come to pass because of natural attrition, the fate of many unfertilised and fertilised ova.

In an address to the 18th International Congress of the Transplantation Society in Rome on 29 August 2000, Pope John Paul II clarified death in the words, "the death of a person is a single event consisting in the disintegration of that unitary and integrated whole that is the personal self". This statement, in defining death, also provided a refinement in the understanding and definition of human life. The implanted, living, human embryo is in the earliest stages of an evolutionary journey which will continue for many years through intrauterine life, infancy, childhood and a variable portion of adulthood. At all stages of its evolutionary journey following implantation in the womb the developing cellular mass is identifiably human, is alive, and possesses the inevitability to realise "... that unitary and integrated whole that is the human self".

The inevitability of human life can only exist, however, with the advent of the spiritual component of the human being, bestowed by God the Creator, since human life does not exist without both a mortal human and an immortal spiritual element (the soul). That inevitability comes with implantation of the blastocyst in the womb, that is with formation of the embryo, a phase lasting by definition for eight weeks into the pregnancy. Thereafter, the life in the womb is known as a foetus. Thus, it can be genuinely argued, that human life does begin at conception, specifically at the time when successful implantation of the blastocyst in the womb occurs and not at fertilisation of the ovum or during its journey to the womb.

With a fuller appreciation of the physiological processes associated with the establishment of pregnancy, the American College of Obstetricians and Gynaecologists in 1972 formally defined conception as implantation of a fertilised ovum in the womb. Science suggests that this definition of conception should be accepted. The implication for contraception is that the moral position should take account of the inevitability of human life with implantation, rather than the potential for human life that attends the processes preceding implantation, namely, fertilisation and the development of the blastocyst. It is reasonable to suggest that if any immorality is to attach to preventing fertilisation by contraceptive measures, that such immorality is different from that which attaches to preventing implantation or destroying an already implanted embryo by contraceptive measures.

The physiological processes of conception raise the question, "If fertilisation does not lead inevitably to human life, is the prevention of fertilisation immoral." The prevention of fertilisation and implantation are fundamentally different, fertilisation representing potential human life, not possessing an individual soul, and implantation representing inevitable human life possessing an immortal soul. This implies that neither a single spermatozoon nor a single ovum possesses an individual spiritual component or soul, a concept analogous with taking an organ from one living person, the donor, and transplanting it in another, the recipient. The organ itself does not embody the soul of the donor, neither does it bestow a new or additional spiritual component on the recipient. The implications of this concept are that fertilisation which bestows only potential life does not include the genesis of an individual spiritual element or soul, while implantation which bestows inevitable life does.

Thus, the fundamental difference between the deliberate frustration of fertilisation and the deliberate frustration of implantation may imply a different gravity of immorality in such actions. In Catholic moral teaching, degrees of gravity in immoral action are expressed in the concepts of venial and mortal sin. The prevention of fertilisation which does not destroy an inevitable human life might properly fit into the venial category, the immorality related to the deliberate attempt to deny the potential for procreation implicit in the sacramental marriage covenant. Once implantation has occurred, however, to terminate that life as a form of contraception equates with abortion and fits the grave or mortal category of sin. Clearly there exists a great difference between the two and perhaps Catholic teaching on contraception should reflect that.

The prevention of fertilisation involves a number of well documented artificial means while the artificial prevention of implantation relies on an intrauterine device (IUD) which prevents implantation by producing hormones unfavourable to the integrity of the womb lining (the endometrium, which nourishes and maintains life in the implanted embryo until full development of the placenta) and by physically damaging the womb lining, both of which render the womb unreceptive to the fertilised ovum. Surgical sterilisation of either man or woman as a contraceptive is an anti-fertilisation measure and thus attracts the same moral consideration as other anti-fertilisation methods. However, it does involve the abandonment of responsible moral stewardship of one's own life in the deliberate risking of that life and in the mutilation of one's own body in unnecessary surgery. It thus incurs a degree of moral transgression elevated above the venial level. Similarly, the pill can be differentiated from the mechanical means of preventing the spermatozoon reaching an ovum (for example, condoms and diaphragms) in that it deliberately interferes with normal physiology which is analogous with un-necessary surgery and thus also carries an added dimension of moral transgression. There is no other situation in which medical practice allows the deliberate prescription of a pill designed to alter normal body function.[26]

---

26 In the early days after its introduction, the pill was responsible for a significant number of serious illnesses and deaths associated with the effects of high levels of hormones well outside the normal physiological range required for normal function. Modifications in the hormone dosages have eliminated much of those side effects in the modern preparations.

None of the anti-fertilisation methods interfere with an already implanted ovum, and thus do not influence the inevitability of human life. Once implantation has occurred the inevitability of human life now exists and this is patently no longer a matter of contraception but a matter of deliberately terminating human life in its inevitable fullness which includes an immortal soul, albeit in the very earliest phases of its inevitable journey to that "... unitary and integrated whole that is the human self". Some IUDs have been modified to carry abortifacient drugs such as ellaOne and orally administered abortifacient drugs such as RU486 and ellaOne are available under the guise of contraceptives. Following implantation, deliberate abortion is the only option to avoid the eventual birth under normal circumstances of a human being in its fullness possessing both human and spiritual components. The IUD and the abortifacient drugs must be considered the contraceptive measures incurring the gravest form of moral transgression.

Any method of contraception within marriage must be evaluated in the light of the Creator God's purpose for sexual union of man and woman. That purpose is the creation of human life through the intermediary of man and woman and is the basis of the sacramentality of Catholic marriage, a covenant between the married couple and God for the purpose of creation of human life. Sexual union within marriage, if it is in accord with the natural moral law, must be open to the creation of human life. Thus any conspiracy to defeat that purpose is contrary to Catholic teaching.

Within marriage, contraception must of necessity take account of the stewardship of any life for which the marriage partners are responsible. That stewardship involves the care for the moral, spiritual and temporal well-being of all children in the family, those living and any future children conceived. This is a responsibility which must be part of the consideration of parents in the decision to use anti-fertilisation forms of contraception balanced against the ability to provide the moral stewardship of parenting. Indeed, it can be argued that the responsibility of parenthood in the interests of the moral wellbeing of the children is a greater moral imperative than producing a child in circumstances wherein the moral stewardship of the child is not possible, when such an event could be prevented by anti-fertilisation means of contraception carrying a lesser moral imperative. The same balance, however, can never be justified if the contraceptive measure used involves abortion of an implanted embryo regardless of the duration or tenure of that embryo in the womb.

Prevention of fertilisation by natural means, the Billings method, enjoys qualified moral approval in Catholic teaching in that it escapes the tag of artificial means contrary to the natural law simply because the identification of ovulation and avoidance of intercourse at the time of ovulation on which the Billings method depends are not by their very nature moral transgressions. Natural means of birth control do, however, demand very concentrated intent and cooperation by both partners in a sexual relationship with the express purpose of identifying ovulation and by avoiding sexual intercourse for some days before and after ovulation occurs. Such conspiracy to defeat God's purpose of creation is equally as contrived as other means of contraception with the sole aim of deliberately preventing pregnancy.

To assume a favourable moral position for the Billings method flirts with fallacy or, more explicitly, embraces it. Indeed, acceptance of a moral position for the Billings method represents a simple Aristotelian syllogistic fallacy, namely: Within sacramental marriage, all contraception [A] is deliberate prevention of pregnancy [B] – All deliberate prevention of pregnancy within sacramental marriage [B] is immoral [C] – therefore, All contraception within sacramental marriage [A] is immoral [C]). The Billings method should logically be considered in the same light as other means of contraception, since the immorality exists in the intention to prevent God's creation covenant with the married couple, not the means whereby that intention is achieved. It is conceded, however, that the Billings method is not an artificial means of contraception contrary to the natural law. Frustrating God's purpose within sacramental marriage using a deliberate and contrived contraceptive method which in itself does not involve any immoral action, if taken in good conscience with a view to responsible parenthood directed towards the moral and temporal wellbeing of any existing or future children, would equally logically seem not to incur a serious moral liability as do other means of contraception when balanced against the imperatives of morally responsible parenting.

While the Catholic Church's teachings against artificial means of contraception cause so much distress for Catholics and attract much attention from its critics, many of whom know little or nothing of the basis of those teachings, the Church does not police adherence or otherwise to its teachings. The Catholic Church, after the example of Christ, its founder, is an instrument of forgiveness, not judgement and condemnation, something that most critics and many Catholics don't appreciate. God, not the Church, will judge the decision that the morally responsible and informed parent has made in a non-contrived conscience. So that conscience on this matter can be informed, however, there is an urgent need for review and clarification of the Church's teaching on the nature of human life and its conception and, most importantly, the establishment of an education commitment to the Catholic laity including the scientific truths revealed in recent times, well beyond the uninformed times when the teachings were implemented.

Contraception is the one, if not the only, identifiable tenet of Catholicism that demands reform or renewal or clearly defined re-affirmation in the modern Church. Any such reform or renewal, however, should certainly reaffirm that artificial means of contraception are inherently immoral since truth is immutable and not a commodity that can be manipulated to meet lifestyle preferences. Some consideration, however, should address the degree of immorality inherent in the use of various forms of contraception, that may be tempered or modified by balancing these against the moral imperatives demanded by responsible parenthood as stated in Pope Paul's encyclical *Humanae Vitae*.[27]

---

27 "With regard to physical, economic, psychological and social conditions, responsible parenthood is exercised by those who prudently and generously decide for serious reasons and with due respect to moral precepts, not to have additional children for either a certain or an indefinite period of time" (*Humanae Vitae*, Pope Paul VI, 1968).

10

STEWARDSHIP OF PROCREATION

The child in the womb is part of my body and
I have the right to decide what I do with my body

The feminist mantra

Ownership – abortion

Hand in hand with the partnership of a human couple with God in the creation of human life comes the obligation to care for the spiritual, moral, and temporal wellbeing of any child born to them. The Catholic notion of the dual nature of human life, spiritual and human, raises the question of ownership of that life and more specifically of each individual living human being. In the modern world the question of ownership of a human life for which a human couple is responsible is poorly understood by many, Catholics and critics alike. The basic scientific truth is that each child is effectively a fifty-fifty product of the mother and father, the only variation being in the gender-determining X and Y chromosomes dependent on the father, not the mother. Male sex is determined by a combination of an X and Y and female sex by a combination of X and X chromosomes. The mother can contribute only an X chromosome to the child and the father either an X or Y. If the father contributes an X chromosome the child will be female and if a Y, a male. Thus, the father alone contributes gender to the child. The paternal ascendancy in determining gender does not bestow greater ownership on the father since both mother and father have contributed equally to the gender of their child, each providing one gender specific chromosome. If a notion of ownership of a child is to be entertained, it is clear and inarguable that the human child is owned equally by both mother and father as far as the element of the human component of that life is concerned. It follows logically that if a decision as to what the fate of that child should be, then father and mother should enjoy equal input into any life determining decisions for the child.

The spiritual component of human life, the soul, is a product, not of the human parents of a child, but of the God Creator. Human life is a product of both the human parent, as intermediary in God's creative process, and God, the spiritual parent. Thus God may indeed also have some ownership rights over that life as the supreme creator. God's ownership of a human life takes primacy over human ownership in Catholic teaching and no human being has exclusive ownership rights over any other human being or over his or her own life. Herein lies the fundamental moral basis within which Catholicism views the tragedies of homicide and suicide and correspondingly, the Catholic condemnation of abortion.

Typical of the feminist abortion lobby mantra is the often repeated inanity, "The child in the womb is part of my body and I have the right to decide what I do with my own body." This implies ownership of the child in the womb exclusively by the woman, excludes any concept of the father's equally shared ownership and any claim by God on human life. With this exclusive ownership comes the right to decide if the child developing in the womb should live or die and the choice to make that decision is also exclusive to the woman. Such is the position of the feminist movement, some political congregations of pro-abortionist politicians in Australia, predominantly from the once Catholic-championed Labor Party, some concerned Catholic renewalists and reformers, and those secular media-based critics ignorant of truth and Catholic teaching. Again, because of a failure to understand, or alternatively ignorance of, the origins of human life, a considerable portion of modern society would appear to deem the child developing in a woman's womb not a human being, but rather some sort of parasitic infestation which threatens the wellbeing of the woman and thus can be legitimately aborted.

The choice to destroy the life in the womb is another frequently repeated mantra of the unthinking pro-choice lobby, a lobby not without its followers amongst Catholic men and women including some deluded clergy, who believe they are supporting the oppressed sisterhood in their compassion, Christian understanding and up-to-date modern education, superior to the medieval thinking of an exclusively male club of celibates who know nothing of human life. Modern America has even been privy to professed Catholics working in abortion clinics in the belief that in so doing they are serving God. Such belief defies understanding and clearly cannot be reconciled with Catholic morality. The sadness is supreme.

Scientific truth unequivocally says that the child is genetically completely different from both the mother and the father and is not part of the body of either of them. The mother's body is but a temporary protective environment for the foetus when it is most vulnerable and incapable of independent life. Further, and importantly, scientific truth recognises that an embryo embedded in the womb is a human life. That is the truth; that is the way it is; that is an unchangeable fact of human life and no amount of created rhetoric can change it. The child in the womb is as much part of its father as it is of the mother. The father has equal rights and responsibilities to that child according to scientific truth. Both, however, if truly human and moral in their determinations, are very much subservient to the Creator God who made them and gave them their own lives. Not to understand that is the height of human ignorance and self-serving pedantry or alternatively, a rejection of the innate understanding of right and wrong and the acceptance of any evil in the quest for personal indulgence.

Catholic teaching on abortion is disarmingly simple. Abortion is a grave moral wrong, represents homicide of the most vulnerable human life, is contrary to the instinctive knowledge of the natural law possessed by all mentally competent human beings and thus, contrary to God the Creator's law. All cogent human beings, regardless of a monotheistic religious adherence or not, Christian or pagan, know that abortion exists only because the product of conception embedded in the womb is living, growing and human. If it were not, there would be no need for abortion. It is the fact that the mother knows that she is carrying the responsibility for another human being who will limit her freedom and demand her responsibility. The mother knows that the inevitability of her pregnancy is a human being. This inevitability is precisely why she seeks abortion. Catholicism can never countenance the destruction of human life and neither can any other adherence claiming a Christian moral code. The controversy that abortion provides in modern Western society is firmly based on obfuscation of self-evident truth in the interest of human lifestyle. It is a great sadness that abortion forms part of the demands for renewal and reform by some Catholic dissidents in the name of the spirit of Vatican II. Such is the inanity of some of those claiming guidance by "the spirit".

The Hippocratic Oath has formed the basis of moral medical practice in the Western world and, although written by a pagan physician ignorant of any Christianity, proclaimed the inherent value of human life and the responsibilities of those entrusted with its care and well-being. The Oath has its origins in the understanding of the natural law, in Catholic teaching embedded by God in the process of creation of the human being. The natural law, in simple terms, is an elemental outcome of the essence of the immortal spirit (soul) exclusive to human life above all other life in this world. The Oath states, "I will give no deadly drug nor perform any operation for a criminal purpose, even if solicited, nor will I suggest any such counsel." It is this short segment of the Hippocratic Oath which has dictated the practice of medicine in relation to the obligation of the doctor charged with the responsibility for human life and, indeed, formed the basis of civil law in Western society regarding medical malpractice, most notably, the practice of abortion.

There is no more poignant insight into the inhumanity of abortion than in the destruction of human life to which so many doctors entrusted with the covenant are now party. But worse is the fact that this destruction is performed in the main by women doctors, driven by women's liberation through the feminist movements around the world. The very cradle of human life, the very instrument without which human creation is impossible, the very life blood of humanity, forms the vanguard of the forces of destruction through their demands that great moral wrongs become their rights. Many women and men have lost the perspective of how uniquely special women are. Without readjustment of that perspective the very cradle of humanity will continue to destroy itself and only barbarism will rise from the ashes of that destruction, the beginnings of which are obvious in the current ethical decline of Western society. It is a great irony that the Hippocratic Oath in its exhortations against abortion arose out of the ascendancy of ancient Greece from barbarism to the pinnacle of civilisation. Perhaps, it is not too unreasonable to suggest that modern Western society's abandonment of that precept heralds the decline of civilisation towards the barbarism from which civilised ancient Greece emerged.

Truth has been abandoned by medical graduates who are abortionists. Their motivation to abort does not come from any altruistic commitment to the covenant of the doctor nor from any compassion for a suffering fellow being or respect for human life. After all, the abortionist fully and consciously intends to destroy human life. The abortionist is a businessman or businesswoman with an academic medical degree who offers no counselling other than to abort. Abortion is the abortionist's income and that income depends on the repetitive marketing of the pragmatic humanist false mantra chanted by those educated to know the truth and instinctively possessed of that truth. The truth will not be abandoned by Catholic teaching which is immutable on the matters of the creation and purpose of human life, regardless of whether or not a majority in a democratic society supports change.

Ethical legislators over a century ago included abortion in the criminal codes virtually throughout Western society and correspondingly so too did Australian legislators. With the loss of ethical principles in the wake of the feminist movement, the criminal codes have been eroded in all states of Australia by socialist Labor governments. Further, at a time when abortion was illegal in all states, the Australian Labor Party through its Universal Health Care Scheme legislation allowed government funding for illegal abortion. New South Wales remains the only state where abortion remains a criminal offence, punishable by sentences of up to 14 years for the procurement or performance of abortion but there is no courage to prosecute under this law. "Legal Abortion", which in NSW can be determined only by the judgement of the court in a matter prosecuted under the abortion law, is freely advertised with impunity in the Yellow Pages business telephone directory in flagrant abuse of the law.

In recent times, the Catholic Church has come under direct challenge of its democratic right to live according to its moral beliefs when the Victorian state government abandoned the criminal abortion law. Under Victorian law, if a child is due to be born tomorrow and is killed in the womb today (full term abortion), that is now legal. If a child is indeed born on the due date, and killed the following day, that is infanticide, punishable by imprisonment. If the child is killed by anyone at any age beyond infancy, that is murder, punishable by imprisonment. If a doctor refuses to kill a child in the womb and refuses to refer the pregnant woman to another practitioner to kill the unborn child, that doctor may be culpable under the law in Victoria. Catholic hospitals may be penalised if they refuse to perform abortion. The legislation also established that a doctor or hospital service can be impelled by law to offer counsel to seek abortion contrary to a moral imperative not to perform abortion and contrary to the outdated Hippocratic exhortation, "I will not perform any operation for a criminal purpose even if solicited nor will I suggest any such counsel." Legislation that is wrong, however, does not convert an evil to a virtue, nor a grave wrong to a human right. Such are the depths to which the law has sunk, based on humanistic abandonment of moral and scientific truth. Such is the destruction of the Judeo-Christian ethic.

The Tasmanian State government in Australia has joined with Victoria in enacting the most regressive and uncivilised pro-abortion laws seen to date in the Western world, which bestow unfettered abortion rights and deny conscientious objection to ethical doctors, a group which includes many and possibly a greater number of non-Catholics than Catholics, who refuse to perform abortion or aid and abet abortion through referral of a woman seeking abortion to an abortionist. At the same time segments of the Western world in the United States and Europe are re-establishing laws to limit abortion. The extraordinary, enigmatic paradox in the actions of the Labor Tasmanian government is that Labor socialist governments in Tasmania have been amongst the world leaders in the preservation of that magnificent dimension of creation which we call the natural environment and yet the very same philosophical government permits the destruction of human life, the greatest of all life on this planet. The hypocrisy defies understanding. The descent towards barbarism and the defacing of civilisation is well afoot in Tasmania, one of the most beautiful natural testaments to the existence of a God Creator in this country.

11

LIFE-CREATING TECHNOLOGY

*It has become appallingly obvious that
our technology has exceeded our humanity*

Albert Einstein

Science – the secular god

The Catholic Church has a paradoxical history in its involvement with science. During medieval times when sorcery, witchcraft and legend carried more credence than science, very few in society were educated or literate. The Church, entirely Catholic at the time, reflected this generalised societal ethos. With the beginning of the renaissance of the later Middle Ages, however, the Church began to alter its perspective, embracing science, and went through a controversial and confused enlightenment which threatened the unity of the Church, not unlike the post-Vatican II era in the modern day Church.

The most celebrated controversy of the time is the widely known dispute with the Polish Catholic priest, Copernicus, in 1543, and almost a century later, Galileo, concerning the nature of our galaxy, in particular, that the sun was the centre of the universe. This claim clashed with the contention at the time that God the Creator, not the sun, was the centre of our universe and that all life on Earth depended on God alone and that the sun had nothing to do with the maintenance of any God-created life. The Church came to accept the science of the relationship of the sun to our planet to the point of its controversial papal establishment of the Gregorian calendar, based essentially on the Earth's rotation around the sun. It was not until 1822, however, that Copernicus's findings were formally declared a physical fact, no longer a hypothesis, and proclaimed as such by Pope Pius VII.

Scientific challenge to God's long held dominion over all in the natural world has continued well beyond Galileo to the present day with such challenges to established belief and teachings as Gregor Mendel's discovery of genetic determination of species characteristics, no longer bestowed individually by God but by genes inherent in all procreative life; Darwin's hypothesis of evolution; the revelation of microscopic bacterial and viral life which debunked disease as a visitation from a wrathful God; the vision of America's first Nobel Prize winner, Alexis Carrel, for human organ transplantation where an organ from a deceased human life could save another human life from death and continue to live and function long after its owner had decayed in his grave; the formation of a human life through in vitro fertilisation technology (IVF). All of these technologies have caused controversy and confusion in our modern world from an ethical or moral perspective. The Catholic Church has again been misunderstood and considered by many to be out of touch with the modern world and to be interfering with human freedoms and rights in applying its teachings to these new technologies.

In Catholic teaching, the same principles of the purpose and sanctified nature of human life apply to all ethical and moral determinations on human life and define the morality that applies in situations made possible by science but outside the purpose of creation and the natural law. Such situations include cloning of human beings; use of stored fertilised ova for medical research as opposed to creation of human life; surrogacy and the use of IVF technology; or any other technology which excludes God's creative purpose or removes it from the God-created natural order. Clearly all of these technologies are facts, just as was Copernicus's hypothesis, and if a God Creator is responsible for all truths and systems on this planet then surely these technologies must be seen as part of God's creation, revealed through scientific research and advancements as an ongoing revelation of God's creation as was, for example, the revelation of the existence of disease-causing bacteria by the microscope. Catholic teaching accepts the truth of these technologies but defines the associated moral responsibility that determines their application to human life. Essentially, the Church teaches that usage outside God's purpose of creation of human life within sacramental marriage is immoral.

Thus, cloning of human beings, surrogacy, homosexual use of IVF to provide a child, or human embryo manipulation as a lifestyle option are not acceptable in Catholic teaching, regardless of any perceived human advantages such manipulations may bring. While such a stand might seem controversial it is certainly not confusing. The confusion that attends Catholic teaching on these matters is the result of lack of education and understanding, not of the impositions of an unsympathetic, ignorant or inhumane Church authority. It must be conceded, however, that in the last 50 years since Vatican II, the Church has failed miserably in educating its people and those ignorant of Catholic teaching who are free, nevertheless, to be damaging critics of Catholicism's application of its moral principles to these new technologies. In this failure, which in large part betrays an unwillingness or more precisely a spinelessness to proclaim its truth in the public domain, unlike Christ in his public life, the Church is highly culpable.

Amongst these new technologies, IVF is perhaps the most controversial, almost certainly because of its success and wide acceptance as a norm in modern society. Essentially, IVF technology involves taking an ovum and a spermatozoon and bringing them together in a laboratory-controlled environment where fertilisation of the ovum occurs and the fertilised cell divides and multiplies into a multi-cellular organism known as a blastocyst which can then be introduced to a woman's womb where under receptive physiological conditions it will implant itself and continue to grow into a full, cognisant human being. The fertilised ovum can also be stored rather than implanted in the womb and held in reserve for future usage, either womb implantation or research. Implantation in a woman's womb, however, means that the multipotential blastocyst is now an embryo[28] and that subject to the same intrauterine, maternal environmental conditions as apply in a naturally implanted embryo, a human being will be the inevitable result. If to conceive is to become pregnant, then conception should properly be defined as implantation of a fertilised ovum (zygote) in a woman's womb. Indeed, this is the accepted definition of conception, clearly established some 40 years ago by the American College of Obstetricians and Gynaecologists.

A zygote stored for future use is strictly not yet an embryo and cannot rationally or logically be considered an extant individual human being and its destruction does not equate with destruction of an implanted embryo (abortion). This latter statement is at odds with currently accepted Catholic teaching and may suggest that this is one aspect of teaching which has been superseded by scientific truth and should be considered for review and clarification by the Church, having consideration of the truth of conception as the origin of human life according to the scientific understanding of what conception is.

Since Catholic teaching confines the process of creation of a human life within sacramental marriage, IVF technology is automatically excluded in any situation outside sacramental marriage, e.g., in surrogacy or homosexual partnership. Within sacramental marriage, where the intention of sexual union is open to the procreation of human life according to God's creative plan, if that intention is frustrated by disease (for example, Fallopian tube disease which prevents the spermatozoon reaching the ovum for fertilisation), IVF

---

28 embryo = human offspring in the first eight weeks from conception (Ref: *Concise Oxford English Dictionary*).

can be genuinely seen as a medical treatment designed for good. (It is understood that the sperm and ovum in this situation come from the marriage partners).

Some Catholic thinking, however, would favour the unacceptability of IVF technology in establishing a pregnancy under any circumstances including within a sacramental marriage with genuine intent to accept sexual love as the instrument of God's creation, not to frustrate that purpose but indeed to promote it. In light of the scientific truth that life begins with implantation in the womb some 6-7 days after fertilisation, it is clear that a stored fertilised ovum does not represent established human life. Catholic teaching on IVF technology, as with contraception, demands review in the upcoming Synod on the family later in 2015. As with contraception, however, the Catholic notion of means justifying a greater moral outcome is a matter for individual informed conscience. Failure to at least review these two aspects of current teaching will bring even further disillusionment with the Church and lead to the alienation of more Catholics. The Catholic Church teaches the morality which defines moral behaviour and forms the basis of an informed conscience. Individual conscience, not the Church, polices moral behaviour. The civil law, not the Church, judges and penalises immoral behaviour which transgresses civil law. God judges immoral behaviour which transgresses his moral law.

12

DEATH AND NEW LIFE

*... death ... the disintegration of that unitary and
integrated whole that is the personal self*
Pope John Paul II, 2000

Euthanasia, organ transplantation

In the face of inevitable death from disease, the Catholic Church imposes no moral or ethical obligation on any human being, doctor, patient or concerned relative, to employ artificial or extraordinary means contrary to the natural order to maintain life. This does not mean, of course, that artificial means available, such as a mechanical ventilator or intravenous feeding, should not be used when there is a prospect of survival. Nor does it mean that doctors and nurses should not employ the means available to them to relieve suffering even when such means, for example, the dose of morphine required to relieve pain, may carry a risk of hastening death. Further, in accord with the concept of God the Creator's primacy of ownership, the termination of human life is for God not the human being to determine and in Christian philosophy is the gateway to a new, eternal, spiritual life reunited with God. This hope for spiritual life after death, an eternal partnership, is one of Christianity's major signatures.

Catholic morality, then, cannot be reconciled with euthanasia in any sense even with the false reassurance of justifying rhetoric such as voluntary euthanasia, humane management, merciful assisted dying, voluntary assisted suicide, all synonyms for mercy killing or compassionate homicide. More apt descriptors than any of the above but deemed politically incorrect in this supposedly enlightened age are the simple, clearly understood words, homicide and murder, punishable under civil law. Neither can the law or medicine in any civilised society sanction euthanasia, since human life and its protection in all circumstances is the prime obligation of both. The decline in our civilisation, however, has brought the barbarians amongst us out of their hiding places with euthanasia being enshrined in legislation in some Western countries, including the Northern Territory in Australia (since repealed). In the face of impending death due to disease, what Catholicism, medicine and the law demand is human compassion and relief of suffering by all means possible short of directly administering a drug intended to kill the sufferer.

Organ transplantation surgery is now a widely accepted norm of modern society but this was not always so. At the beginning of the last century when the visionary Catholic surgeon, Alexis Carrel, proposed that an organ taken from one human being, either living or recently deceased, could be used to save the life of another, it is understandable that this scientific concept alienated him from the Catholic Church in France of that time, an echo of the experiences of Copernicus and Galileo. Carrel was usurping God's role of primacy over life and death, denying death to the donor God-created organ and cheating death in the recipient of the organ transplant. Such a heretical proposition defied the age old understanding of creation and its demise, "Ashes to ashes and dust to dust", and frustrated the Creator's call to eternal life with him in eternity.

Transplantation surgery had caused major controversy and confusion in its implementation as a clinical service over many years beginning in the 1950s and, indeed, the efforts of some ethicists proffering their own views did more than a little damage to patients requiring a transplant. Controversy was resolved in Rome on 29 August 2000, when Pope John Paul II clarified the application of Catholic ethical thinking on human transplantation surgery in an address to The 18th International Congress of the Transplantation Society.

Essentially, Catholic teaching supports human organ transplantation both in the harvesting of organs and the donation of organs, based on an understanding of the prime importance of human life, its dual nature, human and spiritual elements and on the concept expressed in Pope John Paul's words, "... that the death of a person is a single event consisting in the disintegration of that unitary and integrated whole that is the personal self". The simple description of this state of death is "brain death", a situation that can coexist with a beating heart and measurably normal physiological parameters. Catholic teaching defines some practices associated with organ donation as immoral. There is not, however, any defined immorality associated with the transplantation of an organ from one human being to another.

Donated organs come from two sources: one, patients maintained on life support systems in a hospital as part of their treatment following injury or non-communicable disease, in whom death is inevitable as diagnosed because of "... disintegration of that unitary and integrated whole", so-called brain death; and the other, as a donation from a healthy living donor. Donation from a patient on a ventilator is made after the ventilator is switched off and is immoral if performed without confirmation of all those clinical tests which confirm brain death. It is also immoral if carried out without informed consent, either testified to and recorded by the patient prior to the occurrence of those circumstances which led to the clinical state of brain death, or provided with full understanding by the patient's next of kin. Donation from a living, healthy person is more complex and prone to immoral abuse. Donation for a fee or other personal advancement of the donor, trading in organs by third party brokers, or donation as a result of coercion from any source, potential recipient, relative or medical practitioner, are all contrary to Catholic teaching.

Pope John Paul's address to the International Congress of the Transplantation Society has dispelled much of the controversy and confusion that engaged self-professed, home-spun Catholic ethicists in Australia for some years. Some critics of Catholic teaching have drawn attention to the apparent paradox of condemning abortion as immoral and unacceptable under any circumstances at the beginning of life when a cognisant, independent, extra-uterine human being is not yet in existence, and then, accepting the deliberate termination of a human being at the other end of life by removing life support systems and allowing organ donation on the basis of irretrievable, incognisant brain death. In view of the notion of what human life is and means, namely, a unitary and integrated whole, God-created with a dual nature, human and spiritual, then it should be clear that the inevitability of human conception and implantation in a mother's womb is a fully unitary, integrated and cognisant living human being. However, in the case of a human being where that unity and integration no longer exists and the human frame is maintained artificially on a ventilator with forced feeding, and with death inevitable, this is the antithesis of the former, separated by the very same understanding of the nature of human life.

13

THE NEW MILLENNIUM

The joys and the hopes, the grief and anguish of the people of our time, especially of those who are poor or afflicted, are the joys and hopes, the grief and anguish of the followers of Christ as well.

Gaudium et Spes, Vatican II, 1965

Matters of conscience

Gaudium et Spes (Pastoral Constitution of the Church in the Modern World, Pope Paul VI, 7 December 1965) was the last and most comprehensive document promulgated by the Second Vatican Council. It recognised a new era in human history with unprecedented changes throughout society, many of these causing human distress and injustice rather than the emancipation that might be expected if indeed humankind were progressing, not only materially but philosophically and spiritually as well.

This document is best considered as a number of separate documents addressing all aspects of human life and as such is a major social work. In the rapidly changing nature of the developing present day world *Gaudium et Spes* recognises the need for the Church to evolve along with that world in all its dimensions while at the same time not compromising the revelation of scripture and tradition in the definition of Catholic moral teaching. *Gaudium et Spes* (Joy and Hope) defined in this document as "The joys and the hopes, the grief and anguish of the people of our time, especially of those who are poor or afflicted, are the joys and hopes, the grief and anguish of the followers of Christ as well." This simple statement defines the papacy of Francis who clearly sees the grief and anguish of the people of our time, especially of those who are poor or afflicted, as the major thrust of the Catholic Church in the new millennium.

This document indeed summarises the intent of the Second Vatican Council and the obligations of the Church as the body of Christ's people on Earth in the modern world. Although it is hailed as a new vision and has had a profound influence throughout the Christian world, especially in those denominations that constitute the World Council of Churches, *Gaudium et Spes* has not promulgated anything that is foreign or new to Christianity nor to Catholic teaching. Rather, it has highlighted what true Christianity really means and emphasises the practice of Christianity as it applies to all of God's creation, particularly to the human being as the greatest of all creation both at the individual level and also for congregations of human beings as nations. The document is essentially divided into two major sections, each addressing a vast range of the human estate.

Part One embraces the sanctity of human life, the dignity of the human person, the community of humankind, human society and the role of the Church in the modern world. It emphasises the primacy of human beings as the greatest of all creation and the obligations that attend all human beings and human society in dealings with each other and in caring for the world and the relationship between humanity and the Creator God. Part Two reiterates the nature and holiness of family in Christian marriage as a covenant[29] with the God Creator and the obligations attaching to the procreation of human life. More controversially perhaps for a religious declaration, *Gaudium et Spes* expands into the ethics of the political and economic worlds and the obligations of nations in international issues such as war, economic co-operation, populations, work, social and individual rights, social justice for all peoples and the relationship of Church and

---

29 A covenant is best considered in its true meaning as an immutable, everlasting contract.

State. This document, classified as an Apostolic Constitution, enjoys greater authority than a papal encyclical and was supported by 2,309 voting delegates at the Second Vatican Council with 75 against.[30]

It is noteworthy that dissent expressed in the voting on the apostolic constitutions of Vatican II was miniscule. This suggests that there was virtually no meaningful support for reform or renewal in any of the teachings dealt with in these constitutions. However, it is largely the teachings contained in these that drive a vast part of the demands from the modern day reformers and renewalists. In other words, there is little support from Vatican II for the demands for reform and renewal in "the spirit of Vatican II", the catch cry of these people. Should these souls believe that they are indeed guided in their efforts by God in the third personage of the Holy Trinity, the Holy Spirit, then it defies rationality that this same Holy Spirit chose not to inspire and guide his own appointed priests and authority, allowed them to err disastrously, only to then to inspire others, the reformers and renewalists, to implement his true intentions some time later. Some might suggest that the crusade of the reformers and renewalists represents the height of human delusion and self-absorptive pride.

Gaudium et Spes has been seized upon not only by the Catholic world but also by Christianity at large as the blueprint for Christian practice and justice in the modern world and thus has its critics and supporters both. As with all innovation that stimulates enthusiasm, an early exuberant overreaction is not unusual and such was the case with *Gaudium et Spes*. It was to be expected that in its exhortations to care for the poor and in its excursions into the moral demands on politics and economics that it would attract some criticism towards

---

30 The Second Vatican Council promulgated four apostolic constitution documents, the others being *Sacrosanctum Consilium* (The Constitution on the Sacred Liturgy, 1962), voting 2147 for, 4 against; *Lumen Gentium* (The Dogmatic Constitution of the Church, 1964), voting 2151 for, 5 against; *Dei Verbum* (The Dogmatic Constitution on Divine Revelation, 1965), voting 2344 for, 6 against.

the Catholic Church. Australia is one of the most generous of welfare States in the world, dependent both on government through the hardworking taxpayer and increasingly on the generosity of a number of religious agencies such as Catholic Care, Anglicare, Uniting Care and the St Vincent de Paul Society. These agencies carry a large part of the burden of caring for the poor and disadvantaged in Australia and in the third world. They depend on volunteer labour and financial contributions from all Christian Churches as well as from many people, not necessarily Christian, who do not align with any particular Church. Amongst all of these agencies, the Catholic Church is the largest institutional contributor, through its hospitals, schools and aid programs, many of the latter provided at a practical level in the third world by students from its schools in advanced countries such as Australia, the United States and England.

Pope Francis, with his practical experience of working with the poor in South America, has been stigmatised as communistic in some quarters in his urgings for a "preferential option for the poor". His position is in truth far more Christian, in that he proclaims the equality of all humankind regardless of individual riches or poverty. However, the philosophically communistic and militarily armed liberation theology of South America is not easily disconnected from its famous catchcry, the "preferential option for the poor". Pope John Paul II condemned liberation theology and urged that the poor were not to be helped "... by advocating violence or engaging in partisan politics". Such a position was not new in the Catholic Church since Pope Pius XI's 1931 encyclical *Quadragesimo Anno* pointed out that the political systems of Marxist communism, socialism and capitalism were all flawed at their extremes. Such extremes were the antithesis of social justice. In Australia, social justice is dominated by leftist socialism, often proclaiming the virtues of the liberation theology of the preferential option for the poor which has infiltrated existing charitable Christian institutions and agencies to their detriment.

There is no need for Catholicism to proclaim the socialist mantra which smacks to many of frank Marxist communism. Appeals to the presumption that if Christ were alive today he would be a socialist and would support the politics of socialism are ridiculous when he clearly separated politics and religion in his exhortation, "Give to Caesar the things that are Caesar's, and to God, the things that are God's,"[31]

The Catholic position on social justice is unassailably the true Christian position, based as it is on the sanctity of human life, created in God's image. In Australia, however, the response to the teachings and exhortations on social justice proclaimed by Vatican II in *Gaudium et Spes* and by earlier and subsequent papal encyclicals[32] has in some quarters been an overreaction in that it completely ignores the fact that someone has to be an employer and someone has to earn money and provide the wherewithal to financially support social welfare. It further attaches no responsibility to those who depend on social welfare and there is no doubt that there are many abusers of the welfare system essentially stealing from the community at large. Australians are famous for "the government owes me a living" mentality and are no strangers to cheating government systems and charities, so much so, that many, including rich and poor alike, do not see any immorality in such behaviour. Conservative politics is labelled as the immoral player in its attempts to apply financial responsibility in its spending of the Australian people's money and in its identifiable Christianity, while socialist and leftist politics is seen to be the moral standard with its reckless disregard for financial responsibility and abandonment of morality in the promotion of issues such as abortion, euthanasia and same-sex marriage.

---

31 Mark 12:17: "Render to Caesar the things that are Caesar's, and to God, the things that are God's."
32 *Rerum Novarum*, Pope Leo XIII, 1891, and *Quadragesimo Anno*, Pope Pius XI, 1931, established the basis of Catholic social teaching. These have been expanded upon by Popes John XXIII, Paul VI, John Paul II, Benedict XVI and Pope Francis, together with *Gaudium et Spes* and the Synod of 1971.

For Catholicism in Australia, the overreaction which proclaimed a preferential option for the poor and the notion that social justice did not apply to all people, particularly those who were financially well off, disillusioned many who had worked hard, acquired financial independence and were vilified for doing so by the sanctimonious. The social justice hysteria that pervades Catholicism in Australia needs to be seriously curtailed and redirected towards those who are genuinely disadvantaged and need help. There is a great difference between the socialism of love and concern for each other which is the essence of Catholic social justice and the socialism of hate and attrition promulgated by members of socialist governments in this country and converted to an art form by the current generations of the Australian Labor Party.

Imperfections of human nature do exist and should be recognised along with its perfections embodied in the fundamental sanctity of what is God's greatest creation. The imperfections, after all, are precisely the reason why Christ gave his life for all humankind regardless of individual riches or poverty. Christ showed no preferential options in his dying and it is time that some Catholic social justice proponents recognised that. That does not imply, however, that the Church should not speak out against the injustices of greed and self-interest that pervade modern Western society with its idols of self-indulgence and money. It is not the social teachings of the Catholic Church that are at fault. Rather it is the personal interpretations of them in some quarters, often promoted by hypocritical self-interest or personal advancement in a paid job.

14

THE GREAT PARADOX

The evil that men do lives after them
The good is oft interred with their bones

Julius Caesar, Act 3, Sc 2

Humanity: the imperfect perfection of creation

Shakespeare's Juliet searched for her great love in the plaintive call, "Romeo! Romeo! Wherefore art thou, Romeo?" Was Romeo lost, difficult to find, not recognisable or had he failed to deliver on a promise? Since Vatican II, Australian Catholicism suffers all of these obscuring possibilities and might well cry out, "My Church! My Church! Wherefore art thou, my Church?" The bad that followed Vatican II is easy to find in the loss of Catholic identity and overshadows the good, not only for Catholics but also for non-Catholics who at one time admired Catholicism for its moral fortitude even if in disagreement with its dictums.

While the good still exists it accounts for nothing in this modern world which has abandoned its ethics in all aspects of human life and enshrined basic wrongs as human rights. It is almost as if the world is cheering the downfall of the righteous, those sanctimonious do-gooders who attempt to dictate what people can and can't do with their lives based on what is moral and good. Unfortunately such celebration is also a celebration of the downfall of good itself. It is the sort of cheering that might be expected of a victorious army. The general of such an army is certainly not Christ, however, but his enemy whose foot soldiers are those who deride, criticise and seek to destroy Christianity and its moral teachings.

Catholic identity in society is one of Catholicism's great losses in Australia since Vatican II. When something becomes unidentifiable it is ignored. Priests and religious are no longer identified by their dress or public demeanour. The Catholic in the street when he passes a Catholic church no longer bows his head, raises his hat or blesses himself in deference to his God, present in the sanctuary of the church. Silent reverence in Catholic churches, the house of God, has disappeared. The new liturgy resembles the barren nothingness of much of Protestantism and Catholicism is no longer distinguishable in many churches. The Sign of the Cross, a self-blessing, the exclusive signature of Catholicism and Orthodoxy is now seen as a post-score celebration by a sportsman of any persuasion, Christian or not. It no longer identifies a Christian. The Catholic sportsman of yesteryear was famous for his Mass attendance on Sunday, recognised and respected by all his team mates and coaches, Catholic or otherwise.[33]

Such would not be possible in today's crazy world of sports psychology and intrusive, all-pervading training requirements, all more important to Australian sportsmen and sportswomen than spending a short time in prayer and communion with the God who created them. There is no place for God in the Australian sporting world – sport is the god because of the mammon it provides. The world will not see the faith of the Catholic sportsman of yesteryear again in an Australian team unless there is a radical change of attitude, not by society, but by Catholics, who need to reclaim some pride in themselves and their religion. However, for the Catholics of today it

---

33 Before the Rugby World Cup match played between Australia and Ireland in Dublin in 1991, a priest visited the Australian team which contained a high proportion of Catholics and celebrated Mass for the team in their hotel, attended also by the non-Catholic members. In another notable event, the great, undefeated Australian middle distance runner, Herb Elliot, endured a sleepless night before the 1500m final at the Rome Olympics of 1960. At 4.00 am he went to the Pope's daily morning Mass in the Sistine Chapel. Later in the day, having missed out on a night's sleep, he won the gold medal in an Olympic and World record time.

is not difficult to understand that they may not find a lot to be proud of in the modern Church. After all, in the absence of any education in Catholicism they may not know where to look.

Public displays of faith in Eucharistic processions with all the ceremony that attended such events are no longer part of the recognisable face of Catholicism.[34] Church bells calling the people to prayer no longer ring out, challenged by noise minimisation pollution laws. Catholic spokesmen are no longer respected because of their gutlessness to proclaim unfavourable teachings, something contrary to the Australian character, while self-proclaimed Catholic spokespersons in the media have become the official voice of the public Church. Catholic politicians are widely vilified because of their support for traditional Catholic teaching, particularly on matters relating to human life such as abortion, euthanasia, life-creating technology, marriage, sexuality and the objectification of women resulting from the radical feminist movement. And these are just some of the areas where secular recognition of Catholicism no longer exists quite apart from the failings of Catholicism itself which have no doubt inadvertently destroyed identity for its own people through the unnecessary changes implemented in contradiction to the documented determinations of the Second Vatican Council.

It was in the implementation and overreaction to the Vatican II teachings where errors were made, notably in liturgical changes, social justice and education. While the intent of some liturgical changes was

---

[34] It is notable that during the visit of Pope Benedict XVI to Sydney for World Youth Day in 2008 many saw the Stations of the Cross enacted in the streets of Sydney and an open air Mass at Barangaroo for the first time. Both of these events had an amazing effect on secular Sydney with a new awareness of Catholicism, including for many Catholics, with an upsurge in religious practice which was unfortunately very short-lived. Attempts by Church authorities to capitalise on this resurgence of interest failed dismally, lost in the plethora of talk festivals and analyses rather than captured and sustained by true pastoral action. And the downhill slide has continued.

good, in practical terms the outcome has proved very damaging and has destroyed much of Catholic identity. In some places Catholics write their own liturgies, a task sometimes delegated to children attending "children's Masses" during which their doting parents take more photos than they say prayers. Some of these liturgies are guided and directed by teachers not necessarily Catholic. The human in the liturgy would seem to have superseded the divine where it is difficult to recognise the presence of God amongst men in the sacraments of the Catholic Church.

Harm has come from the association of issues of social justice with political socialism which in Australia was once embodied in the Labor Party with its founding values of justice, of concern for the weak, the marginalised and all other human suffering at the hands of an uncaring world. The Labor Party attracted, because of its fundamental concepts of social justice, the vast part of Catholic political support. Today the Labor Party no longer represents the socialism of care and concern for humanity but is devoted entirely to power and gaining that through the voting potential of the self-interested in this world. It associates itself with feminism, same-sex marriage, abortion, euthanasia, sexual liberty and the promotion of self rather than the common good, all very anti-Vatican II positions to adopt. This flies in the face of Christian morality and for the Church to hitch its star to such a wagon is a disillusionment to many faithful Catholics who have abandoned their support for such a party in droves.

There is no doubt that since Vatican II knowledge of Catholic teaching has progressively decreased. Some 90% of young people leaving Catholic schools don't practise the faith and have little knowledge of Catholic teaching. Practice of Catholicism in Australia has decreased from 85% participation at the time of Vatican II to 10% today. Vocations to priesthood and the religious life have fallen disastrously. The prayer life of Catholics is virtually non-existent and the sacraments to many have become secular socialisation rituals attended according to an invitation list and accompanied by partying. Meanwhile false gods pose as Christianity of Christ: the cult of social justice steeped in socialist politics; the cult of self, based on human rights, many of which are indeed moral wrongs; the cult of the dignity of the human person, based on the freedom to do what one desires rather than the sanctity of human life; cults of feminism and gender as great moral determinators; the cult of individual spirituality and the cult of eugenics.

Educational counters to this for Catholic people and particularly the young are difficult to find and are by no means universal within Australian Catholicism. All of these are the antithesis of the intent of the Second Vatican Council as documented in *Gaudium et Spes* which has failed through misinterpretations of its intent to produce universal good but rather, in the greatest of paradoxes, has seemingly produced much that is bad.

For the Catholic laity, the changes that came with Vatican II have resulted not in the perceived good envisaged in the true spirit of the Council. The loss of the sacred liturgy, the assumption by the laity that they are now a moral authority that must be heard, the widespread criticisms and trashing of papal authority, the accelerating failure to follow the moral teachings and practice of the Church, the abandonment of meaningful Catholic education and the secularisation of religious life are all due to the failure of the local Church to establish the Council's true spirit. This failure lies entirely with the bishops and represents the destruction of identity within Catholicism itself, simply because of reliance on the human rather than the divine, disguised under mountains of rhetoric, meaningless to the common man. The environment which has arisen has allowed the apostate religious and clergy and the armies of reformers and renewalists to continue to trash the genuine reforms of Vatican II to suit their preferences, all in the name of the Council's "spirit". Vatican II is over. Its promulgated teachings require no further modification, although the damage from overreaction to some of those teachings does need repair and restoration. It is time for the wolves in sheep's clothing of biblical record (Matt. 7:15,16) to be dealt with and consigned to wherever they belong, which is not in the Church instituted by Christ unless they are prepared to embrace that Church in its fullness.

However, hand in hand with the bad is the resounding good both of Catholicism and Vatican II. Again according to Shakespeare's enduring wisdom, expressed by a thespian Mark Anthony, "The evil that men do lives after them. The good is oft interred with their bones" (*Julius Caesar:* Act 3, Sc 2). It is easy to see the bad and be critical of it as in what is written here, but such can never be accepted without acknowledgment of the good and an attempt to discern the balance between the two.

Vatican II reaffirmed the inherent sanctity of human life and the equality of all humankind, regardless of race, belief and material possessions. This recognition was reflected in its determinations on racism, refugees, the inherent goodness in other religions including those that are not Christian, its ecumenical aims for the unification of Christianity in the one Church and a commitment to justice for all peoples and nations in its social justice objectives.

In practical terms, Catholicism remains the largest private institutional contributor to the poor, the sick and the disadvantaged both in Australia and worldwide, serving millions of such people every day. The Church is Christian, bears no ill will to anyone but sometimes entertains either the naivety of innocence or the fear of criticism which does it enormous harm as well recorded in the sexual abuse scandals of recent times.

But in the midst of all the good there is the bad and therein rests the great paradox. Vatican II set out to enhance the good in the new millennium but rather than achieve that it produced a Church of conflict destroying much of its goodness. Universality (catholicity) has been lost and the Church is now made up of multiple self-interested factions or feuding tribes believing their interests are what Vatican II intended while ignoring papal authority. Shakespeare's words expressed by Mark Anthony all those years ago came from an understanding of human nature in all its greatness and imperfections. The bad will not be forgotten for a long time and the good will not be seen and perhaps buried in the past unless these factions return to their roots as people in Christ. These need to abandon the indulgence of the supposed benefits of the world, the pretend university degrees, the conferences and the political excursions, in favour of the religious life commissioned by Jesus of Nazareth.

15

THE HEALING

*In society and the world in which we live
selfishness has increased more than love for others*

Pope Francis

Love: healer of the deepest wounds

An assessment of the half century following the Second Vatican Council indicates that, in the main, the Council was a good thing of brave intent which unfortunately brought not the rejunvenated Catholic Church of the modern world as envisaged by Pope John XXIII. Sadly, it brought much disruption, dissatisfaction and destruction. These negative outcomes have arisen not from the pronouncements of the Council as expressed in the Vatican II documents but by the interpretations of those documents and also perhaps by lack of planning in preparation for the liturgical changes which required a revised catechism and daily missal, both essential to the education of Catholic people in the new millennium Out of these deficiencies has grown a protest movement with two proponents, a small, largely ineffective faction of conservative restorationists and the large, irrational and destructive vocal faction of anti-conservative reformers who continue to wreak unnecessary havoc in their interpretation of "the spirit of Vatican II".

These two groups reflect a very large part of the post-Vatican II Church, the disillusioned (the restorationists) and the disappointed (the reformers and renewalists). A third post-Vatican II group, rarely heard in the public domain and widely dismissed by the other two, has remained faithful to the papacy and Catholic teaching while accepting the prescribed changes that followed the Council and continuing to live as practising Catholics in the Catholic Church of the modern era. They are not controversial and thus are never heard or canvassed for an opinion by the opponents of Catholicism. Unlike with the reformers, renewalists and a coven of lay, self-proclaimed Catholic spokespersons in the secular media, celebrity is not their pursuit.

The restorationists, who live in the pre-Vatican II Church of the past, perceive the vast part of the changes that followed Vatican II to be wrong and clamour for complete restoration of the pre-Vatican II Church. Such demands are equally as flawed as those of the reformers but, in contrast, will not endure. Unlike the reformers the majority of whom never experienced the pre-conciliar Church and have no benchmark other than their own agendas to guide them, the restorationists are a passing breed limited by their human mortality. The reformers, however, are unlikely to simply fade away and seemingly possess no intention to forgive past administrative inadequacies, mistakes or scandalous indulgences.

Reformers are made up of identifiable groups, often overlapping with each other. The combined reform lobby includes those who wish to take the responsibility for the teaching of moral law and administration of the Catholic Church away from a central, scholarly authority and thus bestow greater authority on the laity; opponents of an authoritative papacy; disillusioned ex-nuns and women who want to be priests, seduced by the mantra of feminism; people who want change in the Church's moral position on abortion, contraception, euthanasia and sexual licence, both homo- and hetero-sexual; proponents of same-sex marriage, married clergy and the ordination of women to the priesthood; feminists who demand all or some of the above; concerned men of dubious motivation who feel the need for solidarity with their sisters; some Catholic clergy possessed of a perception of the primacy of their exclusive understanding as opposed to all others; collections of lay theologians and common or garden self-styled intellectuals who don't like to be told what they should believe or practise by any authority, religious or otherwise, including Christ himself through holy scripture. These reformers are distinguished in that their claims have no basis whatever in the published determinations of the Second Vatican Council.

Effectively, these groups of reformers, some of them formalised in associations with a defined objective, mission statement and membership lists, represent factions or tribes opposed in some way to the established system from which they arise, in this case the Catholic Church. Factionalism is very disruptive of unity, stagnates progress and destroys the unifying identity of the whole. It has the inherent capacity to ignore change or modifications in its own agendas and thus to generate internal conflict. This is evident in the Australian Catholic Church and will continue to inflict great damage on the Church adding fuel to the inferno lit by the uninformed secular opponents of any form of Christianity, particularly that which decries moral degradation in modern society.

While the reformers cry out in the name of Christianity they in fact deface and tear apart true Christianity by their attacks on the Christian Church instituted by Jesus Christ. Many are no doubt seemingly good people but perhaps too naive to understand that they are the instruments serving the destruction of Christ's Church on Earth, equally as culpable as those priests who abandoned their God to follow the path of the sexual revolution in the most diabolical of all sexual abuses. These factional reform groups are the very antithesis of the intentions and spirit of the Second Vatican Council. Why they continue to torture themselves is an enigma when all they need do is leave the Catholic Church and join one of the many Protestant Churches which already embodies their desires. Unless, as it sometimes seems, their true intention is to destroy the Catholic Church

There is, however, a need for both some restoration and some reform or renewal in the Church. The sacred liturgy is perhaps in most need of restoration. While the vernacular should be retained, it frequently fails to inspire and in a multicultural and multilingual society like Australia fails in the assimilation of a non-English speaking migrant population who often can find no community in their own Catholic Church. Ministries in languages other than English do exist in Australia but these tend to isolate those who depend on these languages from the English speaking Church and equally isolate the English speaking Australian community from migrant communities. Universality (catholicity) is correspondingly lost and it is doubtful that it will ever be regained in the living of Catholic life in a faith based community, foreign because of language isolation, even though the universality of moral teaching remains. If, however, a culturally neutral language such as Latin were restored this problem would be eliminated. Individual tribes, separated by language and culture, would again become part of a universal whole, free to print their own bilingual missals with their preferred vernacular alongside the universal Latin. It is probably too late to correct the great fragmentation brought about by the loss of a universal Church language and any attempt to restore a universal language might now be counter-productive but should be considered.

Sacred music, however, is capable of uniting people and elevating the human spirit towards God regardless of the language of any accompanying vocals. Herein resides the one major area where both restoration and reform are urgently needed. Local churches would do well to heed the Council's pronouncements on sacred music both in instrumentation and vocals as addressed in the document *Sacrosanctum Concilium*. In certain liturgical situations there is still a place for those vocals and uplifting music common to many religions, Christian and otherwise, which inspire a sense of reverence and awe. Music affects different human emotions. Rock music and dixieland jazz, for example, create a very different emotion from reverence for God and should have no place in the sacred liturgy (as has happened in

Australia on occasions) even though they bring people together acting as one, regardless of the accompanying language. Some would argue that all forms of music and song come from God's gift to certain individuals and thus represent praise for God in the use of that talent in the liturgy. Such, however, is not the essence of sacred music which is to elevate the human spirit towards God, where praise and awe of God is the essence of the human response to the music, rather than a toe-tapping trance which pleases the psyche of the participants or praises an individual human talent.

In a different culture jazz music can be sacred, uplifting towards God, as seen in the African-American spiritual music of the southern states of America, the so-called negro spiritual genre. In many cultures sacred chanting, such as Gregorian chant in Catholicism, and different instrumentals such as, say, the didgeridoo of the Australian aboriginal people and the bongo drum of the African people, are very potent instruments of elevation of the human spirit. The Second Vatican Council acknowledged the potency of the spiritual elements that define different cultures and this needs to be reaffirmed in a Western country such as Australia where, perhaps, the guitar, the bongo drum, the honky-tonk piano or the violin may not have the same effect of elevation of the human spirit towards God as might the grand organ.

Another pressing need in the modern Catholic Church is the restoration of reverence for God in Catholic churches. The church is not a community meeting hall. It is the house of God. While it is integral to Catholic community, it is essentially there to give praise to God and represents the formal meeting place of God amongst his people in the sacraments. It houses the Holy of Holies, God on Earth in the consecrated host. It is long overdue in the post-conciliar Church that this fact is again acknowledged and that people behave appropriately in the presence of God in his house which is not the place for playing happy families or a forum for catching up on last week's gossip. Unnecessary social chit-chat, lack of reverence in the procession to receive the consecrated host in Holy Communion and the accompanying inane hymn singing should be eliminated. If ever there was a place for sacred music elevating people towards their God it is in the Eucharistic procession to receive the consecrated Host in Holy Communion with God. It is impossible to imagine anyone invited to visit the Queen of England in Buckingham Palace carrying on in her presence in the way so many Australians carry on in the presence of their God and Creator in Catholic churches. In a word, such behaviour is, at the very least, a disgraceful lack of courtesy and respect.

The call to prayer in Christian communities, by no means peculiar to Catholicism but to all Christian denominations and indeed throughout Islam and Buddhism, was a great proclamation to the world at large of God's presence on this Earth. This practice is still widely accepted in European Christian communities and causes no societal unrest. In Australia, however, this Christian signature has been generally abandoned by Catholicism. A return to the identifiable and unifying influence of the call to communal prayer (seen a number of times a day in Islamic communities and accepted by Australian residents living in such areas) that the rung Angelus and the church bells heralding the beginning of daily morning Mass once provided should be restored for no purpose other than to raise awareness once more of God in this world. In Australia's big cities, Sunday church bells and carillons still peal forth, not as a call to prayer it seems, but as a tourist attraction. More importantly, the re-establishment of a communal devotional prayer life is a great need. Currently, not all devotional prayer life is shared in the day to day Church but rather serves small groups with a particular interest. The prayer life of Lent based on reconciliation and self-denial through alms giving and fasting should be actively pursued. The Islamic faith manages this during Ramadan as do the Eastern and Orthodox Churches during Lent. Surely Catholicism is not too precious to do likewise. It did, after all, introduce these practices to the world at large.

The most urgent need of all is the restoration of education in both children and adults. The inanity of the mantra, "parents are the prime educators of their children", used by those entrusted with the religious teaching of Catholic children to escape their responsibilities and dash off in pursuit of secular fame in political protest, social justice activism and overseas missions, all in the name of the spirit of Vatican II, has to be abandoned. Clearly, relying on it has failed whole generations of young Catholics with statistics indicating that up to 90% of young nominal Catholics leaving Catholic schools do not practise the faith and have huge deficits in their knowledge of Catholic teaching. Many of those members of religious orders have abandoned their teaching of Australian children to join the post-Vatican II "new evangelisation" in missions overseas where they enjoy an ego-boosting captive audience, while the Australian Church's greatest and neediest mission field is in this country within the Catholic community itself. There is, however, no captive audience in Australia and the work is hard. In Australia, with its traditional larrikinism, a missionary is likely to be advised in language not too savoury to take his missionary zeal elsewhere and dispose of it in an uninhibited, unbecoming manner somewhere unseen in his person.

Education, both of children and adults, is the necessary foundation for the re-emergence and restoration of the Catholic Church in Australia and from it will flow automatically all the good things urged in *Gaudium et Spes* for the living of a true Catholic life. Australia in the post-Vatican II era has established its first Catholic universities and surely it must be their primary aim to enhance the Catholic education of Catholic people not evident to date despite the constructed mission statements that have become compulsory and serve as the definitive commitment to education in the name of Catholicism. The time is long overdue that the fleets of religious, the erstwhile teachers of the Catholic faith to children who have ignored that ministry and the mission fields of this country, need to abandon their comfortable conferences and pursuits of worthless qualifications and return to the education of the young which would serve Catholicism and their Christ far more effectively.

Insomuch as it deals with the restorationists, whose cause is certainly doomed and will not survive, and the reformers whose vision for the future is shadowed in gloom unless their views and demands are met, what is written here might easily be seen as an epistle of doom and gloom for the Catholic Church both in Australia and worldwide. Such an appraisal is of course quite valid when no account has been taken of the surviving Catholic Church characterised by that third group of post-Vatican II Catholics who have responded to the true spirit of the Council, have embraced the good in the changes, accept the primacy of papal authority as instituted by Christ himself, and have remained faithful to Church teaching and practice. Unlike the restorationists and reformers they are the Catholic Church, the body of Christ, and will survive until the end of time as promised by Christ.

Finally, there is a great need for reform of the administrative processes practised in the Vatican. Such reforms are not of a primary moral nature but purely of the business model. Some of the clamour for reform confuses this with a need to alter papal authority in matters of fundamental Catholic moral teaching. Such is of course ridiculous and has nothing to do with Vatican II. The papacy of Francis has already been distinguished by administrative change, not pleasing to some of the erstwhile unopposed powerbrokers in the Vatican. The path for change has been set. Now the time has come to support the papacy, not destroy it. The Church has finally found a way towards healing in this Pope. Therein resides the true spirit.

As with most things that disturb a long established status quo, balance and harmony in response to the change is the only solution free of damage. It is this harmony, not division, that the modern Catholic

Church desperately needs, accepting the authority and guidance of the papacy, re-affirmed and insisted upon by Vatican II, and ensuring, as exhorted by Pope John XXIII when he convened the Council, that fundamental Catholic doctrine would not be compromised in the quest to accommodate modern society's demands for the liberation of personal moral responsibility. Healing will not happen while the reformers continue to press their demands ignoring the true spirit of Vatican II in blatant disrespect for papal authority and the established teachings of the Church, particularly those that relate to the morality of marriage, sexuality, the family, procreation, abortion and euthanasia; that is, the living of human life.

The New Testament is the most widely published, read and quoted book in the history of the human race. It is the greatest love story ever written. It is the story of the overwhelming love of Jesus of Nazareth, the Christ, for his fellow human beings, a love steeped in acceptance of human frailty and imperfection and the willingness to forgive. It is a love that did not exclude his teaching against the immoralities of the world in which he lived, since such immoralities defaced the innocence of the greatest of all his creations, his greatest artwork, humanity. It is a love that stands in stark contrast to the reluctance of the modern day Australian Catholic clergy to speak out against the immorality and apostasy of the world in which we live.

It was not a love that damned, but a love that healed both physically and spiritually. As this hero of the story suffered cruelly at the hands of his torturers, he did not condemn. He forgave them in his dying breath. "Forgive them, Father", he prayed, "for they know not what they do".[35] Herein rests the Christian example, the essence of love, the healing. Herein rests a powerful message for the cacophonous, would

---

35 Luke 23:34: Jesus of Nazareth's extraordinary expression of forgiveness, regardless of the enormity of human wrongdoing, uttered during the torture of his execution by crucifixion.

be reformers, for the armies of critics and apostate laity who plague today's Catholic Church: Divest yourselves of intellectual pride and self-righteousness and find the way to both love and forgiveness – for Christ's sake. Then and only then will true healing come.

16

"Such is Life"

The last words of Australia's feted heroic outlaw and Irish Catholic rebel

Edward (Ned) Kelly

The law: maker and breaker

Civilisation, the ordering of human society towards harmony, free of all manner of conflict between human beings, is fundamentally embodied in, driven and sustained by civil law, conceived in the main to protect human life in all its aspects from the interpersonal dealings of people of all creeds, colours and nationalities, to caring for the environment in which we live, or driving a motor vehicle responsibly and everything in between. The development of law and the advance of civilisation are interdependent and neither can evolve without the other.

The evolution of civilisation has also been associated with advances in life preservation and protection of human life in the practice of medicine, in the elevation of the human spirit through education and the moral guardianship of the sanctity of human life by Christianity. So much so, that in our society these four, law, medicine, education and divinity are recognised as the learned professions, occupations in which the practitioners serve human society before their own needs, even if necessary without a fee, the very antithesis of what current civilisation considers to be professional practice.

In Western civilisation, the way of life and the law evolved within a

Christian framework. Although that framework was beset with dispute between groups of human beings ordered together in different and conflicting man-made religious denominations, the central theme of Christianity, belief in a creator God embodied on Earth in God-become-man, Jesus of Nazareth, was the unifying influence that determined the rise and extraordinary achievements of Western civilisation. "With rise", cautions the adage, "comes the fall".

For the last century or so Western society has progressively abandoned the very foundation of its being, the Judeo-Christian ethic, seduced by power, greed and the expansion of fundamental human wrongs into the realm of rights. This decline has accelerated since the Second World War where military might and power have transcended truth and knowledge; where Jefferson's immortal declaration has become meaningless in the face of human greed; where we have dismantled education in favour of economically based job training; where individualism supplants the common good; where not all human beings are considered equal; where the sanctity of human life is subservient to humanist self-interest; where women have been seduced by the feminist movement and lost a sense of how very special they really are; where we have forgotten how special every human being is; where we can no longer see the greatness of human creation in our fellow human beings or the natural world around us.

Western civilisation is descending into the barbarism that the ancient Greeks overcame so long ago. The supreme sadness, however, lies in that the law, the great protector of human life and genuine rights, as envisaged in the spirit of Jefferson's immortal declaration and in Hippocrates' covenant with humanity, is the very vehicle which is destroying civilisation and championing barbarity.

When Judge Redmond Barry placed the black cap on his head and pronounced the sentence of "hanging from the neck until dead" on Edward (Ned) Kelly for the crime of destroying a human life, the outlaw simply commented with typical Irish, maudlin fatalism, "Such is life". But not any more.

> *Come, Catholic Australia,*
> *so sadly led astray.*
> *Did you not hear Him say,*
> *"I am, my child, the truth.*
> *I am the life, the way."*

A Last Word

This year, 2015, marks the 50th anniversary of the conclusion of the Second Vatican Council. Since the advent of Pope Francis, the tempestuous sea of Catholicism, stirred by the perceived failings of the papacies following the Council to implement what many believed to be the reforms necessary to serve Catholicism in the modern world, has fallen calm. The clamour has become an increasingly distant echo. The overriding interpretations of the Council documents by reformers and proponents for renewal were that the Church return to the Christianity of Christ's time on Earth and that authority in matters of faith and morality not be solely embodied in the papacy, but determined by the people of the Church in a form of communal agreed philosophy serving the human rather than the divine and derived from little authority other than numerically equal gender representation.

If indeed the cacophonous reformers and proponents for renewal have been seeking the guidance of the "spirit "they claim inspires them, then they need seek no more. In Pope Francis, the man, the embodiment on this Earth of the spirit of Jesus of Nazareth shines forth like a beacon lighting the way for all peoples to see. Here is a man who shuns opulence, walks amongst his people teaching them as Christ did, sharing their sorrows and joys, sharing a meal with the poor and washing the grime and hopelessness from their faces, providing comfort for those whom comfort has long abandoned. Here is a man who brings hope and joy. Here is the embodiment of the most important of the Vatican II determinations enunciated in the document *Gaudium et Spes* (Joy and Hope). The spirit of the Church of Jesus of Nazareth is renewed, is restored. The cause for reform and renewal should be no more. The time has come for the people, the

Church, to unite with and support this Pope and his papacy including acceptance of the authority of the papacy, to truly live the life of Christ and to abandon self-righteousness. Only then will we see the fruits of Vatican II: a renewed and vibrant Church steeped in humility and love for all humanity.

AUTHOR PROFILE

John Frawley AM, Honorary Consultant Surgeon and Emeritus Head of Vascular and Transplantation Surgery at Prince of Wales and Sydney Children's Hospitals in the University of New South Wales and Emeritus Consultant in Vascular Surgery at Sydney A ventist Hospital, is a Catholic father, grandfather, author, poet and lecturer on human life issues in the public domain. He has been honoured through investiture in the Order of Australia as a pioneer in kidney transplantation and vascular surgery in adults and children, by awards for distinguished service, through tree plantings in the B'nai B'rith Forest of Peace in Israel, and by inclusion in *Marquis Who's Who* in the World and *Who's Who in Medicine and Healthcare*.

His publications include a large body of peer reviewed scientific papers and book chapters in the surgical world literature, a little poetry and theology, articles and commentary on human life ethics in the secular and religious press and the books, *Some Horses have Purple Legs: Occasional recollections of a lucky boy* (Shining Press, Sydney, 2007), a childhood memoir, and *A Surgical Life: Dreaming things that never were* (Copyright Publishing, Brisbane, 2011), a creative non-fiction, historical memoir.

www.ingramcontent.com/pod-product-compliance
Ingram Content Group UK Ltd.
Pitfield, Milton Keynes, MK11 3LW, UK
UKHW021300180426
11947UKWH00015B/932